# Plan the Perfect
# WEDDING
## ON A SMALL BUDGET

From
# WedSpace.com
The Fastest Growing Bridal Community
and Wedding Planning Website

**Written by America's Top Wedding Experts**
Elizabeth & Alex Lluch
Authors of Over 3 Million Books Sold!

WS Publishing Group
San Diego, California

Plan the Perfect Wedding on a Small Budget

By Elizabeth & Alex Lluch
America's Top Wedding Experts

Published by WS Publishing Group
San Diego, California 92119
Copyright © 2011 by WS Publishing Group

Cover photos:
Karen French
www.karenfrenchphotography.com

For Inquiries:
Log on to www.WSPublishingGroup.com
E-mail info@WSPublishingGroup.com

Printed in China

ISBN: 978-1-936061-26-6

# CONTENTS

# CONTENTS

# Introduction

YOU MUST BE VERY EXCITED TO HAVE found that special person with whom you will share the rest of your life. And you must be looking forward to what will be one of the happiest days of your life — your wedding! Planning a wedding can be fun and exciting, but it can also be overwhelming; that's why WedSpace.com created *Plan the Perfect Wedding on a Small Budget.*

*Plan the Perfect Wedding on a Small Budget* contains worksheets, checklists, timelines and comparison charts to keep you organized and on top of your wedding plans.

This book begins with a detailed wedding planning checklist containing everything you need to do or consider when planning your wedding and the best timeframe in which to accomplish each activity.

Next, a detailed budget analysis lists all the expenses that are typically incurred in a wedding. In this book, you'll find everything you need to know about each aspect of the wedding, including Options,

Things to Consider, price ranges and more.

Most important, *Plan the Perfect Wedding on a Small Budget* contains extensive tips and ideas for saving money on every aspect of the wedding, including advice from real couples and their wedding experiences.

At the end of each chapter you'll be treated to a full-color section of a real couple's wedding, including their total amount spent, size and location of their wedding, and a breakdown of their budget and how they saved, splurged and prioritized. From DIY projects to negotiating tips, to asking for help from friends and family, let these real couples, with budgets of $2,000 to $10,000, be your inspiration for a beautiful, wallet-friendly wedding.

We are confident that you will enjoy planning your wedding with the help of *Plan the Perfect Wedding on a Small Budget*. Also, if you know other Options, Things to Consider, or Ideas to Save Money, or if you are interested in submitting your real wedding under $10,000 to be included in a future edition of this book, please write to us at: WS Publishing Group; 7290 Navajo Road, Suite 207; San Diego, California 92119 or email info@ WSPublishingGroup.com.

We will include your ideas and suggestions in our next printing. We listen to brides and grooms like you — that is why WS Publishing Group has become the best-selling publisher of wedding planners!

Sincerely,

Elizabeth H. Lluch

# Wedding Events at a Glance

YOUR WEDDING WILL BE A CELEBRATION that will most likely span several different events. From the moment you get engaged to your last dance, your wedding will be filled with many special occasions.

Use the following worksheets to easily keep track of events, dates, locations, and contact information. Keeping these details in one place will help you plan ahead for each party and quickly reference important information.

Once you have finalized all of your events, make copies of these worksheets and distribute them to members of your wedding party, consultants, or vendors who would require this information.

# WEDDING EVENTS AT A GLANCE

## Engagement Party Date:

Engagement Party Time:

Engagement Party Location:

Contact Person:                    Phone:

Website:                           E-mail:


## Bridal Shower Date:

Bridal Shower Time:

Bridal Shower Location:

Contact Person:                    Phone:

Website:                           E-mail:


## Bachelor Party Date:

Bachelor Party Time:

Bachelor Party Location:

Contact Person:                    Phone:

Website:                           E-mail:


## Bachelorette Party Date:

Bachelorette Party Time:

Bachelorette Party Location:

Contact Person:                    Phone:

Website:                           E-mail:

## Ceremony Rehearsal Date:

Ceremony Rehearsal Time:

Ceremony Rehearsal Location:

Contact Person:                              Phone:

Website:                                     E-mail:


## Rehearsal Dinner Date:

Rehearsal Dinner Time:

Rehearsal Dinner Location:

Contact Person:                              Phone:

Website:                                     E-mail:


## Ceremony Date:

Ceremony Time:

Ceremony Location:

Contact Person:                              Phone:

Website:                                     E-mail:


## Reception Date:

Reception Time:

Reception Location:

Contact Person:                              Phone:

Website:                                     E-mail:

# WEDDING PLANNING NOTES

# Christie & Brandon

Total Spent: $6,500
**May 16, 2010 • Frisco, Texas • 140 guests**
**Photography by Celina Gomez, www.celinagomez.com**

## Budget Breakdown

| | | | |
|---|---|---|---|
| Attire | $456 | Bar | $0 |
| Stationery | $102 | Music | $0 |
| Ceremony Site | $600 | Bakery | $200 |
| Photography | $2,864 | Flowers | $345 |
| Videography | N/A | Décor & Rental Items | $521 |
| Reception Site | $475 | Miscellaneous | $535 |
| Food | $300 | **Total** | **$6,500** |

When it came time to plan their lovely Texas wedding, Christie and Brandon had tons of terrific money-saving ideas. "We chose to have a smaller budget because we didn't want to get carried away with an extravagant wedding; we wanted to focus on a great marriage," says Christie. Things like renting a gorgeous wedding gown, hand-making bridesmaids' bouquets, and printing invitations at home left room for splurges on the venue and photography. Delicious catered barbecue at the rehearsal dinner gave guests a taste of Texas, while the couple created a decadent dessert-only wedding reception (dessert is everyone's favorite part of a meal anyway!).

## FROM THE BRIDE

The venue and photography were the most important decisions, and thus our biggest splurges. We picked the Historic Lebanon Baptist Chapel, a beautiful, fully refurbished historic chapel with wooden pews and stained glass windows, which saved us on decorating costs. In addition, the chapel is owned by the City of Frisco, which saved us on rental costs. Privately owned facilities are much more expensive. We also got married on a Sunday, which saved us $300.

## ATTIRE & BEAUTY

I rented my wedding dress for $50 and spent $64 on alterations, so I saved hundreds or even thousands of dollars on the gown. My shoes were from DSW, and were just $7 because I had a gift card and a $10 coupon. Other accessories, such as my veil from David's Bridal, garter from Oriental Trading Company, and jewelry from Target, were inexpensive, simple and beautiful. I did my own hair and went to Dillard's for my makeup, which was free, although I bought $50 worth of makeup products to use at the wedding and after. The groom's tux cost a small $40 rental fee and his tungsten wedding band was just $60 from Overstock.com!

The bridesmaids dresses were $25 each. I bought them at JCPenny, and they were my gift to my bridesmaids. Everyone thought they were very cute.

## STATIONERY

We bought invitations at Walmart and printed them at home. Sending RSVP cards with the invitation is a tradition that can easily be tossed out! We used a free wedding website for guests to RSVP, instead of paying for stamps for the return envelopes. Then, we used the RSVP cards that came with the invitations as thank-you cards. We also made 150 programs and had them printed at Kinko's.

## PHOTOGRAPHY

With photography, I think you get what you pay for. I met with four different photographers, starting with those whose packages were the least expensive. After viewing all their work, it was very clear that Celina Gomez was the most expensive but by far the best.

## FLOWERS

I'm also a huge proponent of do-it-yourself projects. We saved a ton of money by making our own bridesmaids' bouquets and groomsmen's boutonnieres with silk flowers two months prior to

the wedding. No one could tell the difference. And if brides want real flowers, they are just as easy to DIY, too.

### DÉCOR

For my bouquet and reception table decorations, we bought flowers from Kroger and saved nearly $250. We also purchased votive candles from Walmart at $.59 a piece.

### FOOD

We had a dessert buffet at our reception instead of a sit-down meal and made all the food ourselves the day before. We had brownies and cupcakes, cheesecake bites, strawberry shortcake, banana pudding in plastic martini glasses, and an ice cream sundae bar with all the toppings. We also served lemonade, tea and punch.

### MUSIC

For ceremony music, our friend played the piano and sang and his friend played the cello. He even composed a song for us. At the reception, another good friend, who attends Toastmasters regularly, was our DJ and MC, for free. I wrote the script and put the music we wanted on our iPod.

### ADVICE

Brides should think about the traditions they can live without to reduce costs. You don't have to follow wedding traditions just because everyone else does.

For instance, "the groom can't see the bride until she walks down the aisle" is a wedding tradition that brides should consider ignoring if they splurge on photography. Ask your photographer about a "First Look," where your photographer captures you and the groom seeing each other for the first time before the ceremony. Then there is plenty of time for intimate portraits of the happy couple that might not otherwise be possible following the ceremony.

Wedding favors are another example of a wedding tradition that brides don't have to follow. We spent too much money on candy that no one ate, not to mention the time we wasted stuffing tiny bags with ribbons that were extremely hard to tie! Instead, consider printing an engagement session portrait for your guests. Create a free account at Shutterfly.com; they always email incredible specials, such as "75 free 4x6 prints."

True, I had moments when I wished I would have spent a little more on flowers or wished I would have purchased chair covers, but honestly, when the big day arrived, I didn't even notice or care. I was just thrilled to have all my friends and family together.

# Budget Analysis

THIS COMPREHENSIVE BUDGET ANALYSIS HAS been designed to provide you with all the expenses that can be incurred in any size wedding, including such hidden costs as taxes, gratuities, stamps, and other items that can easily add up during a wedding.

After you have completed this budget, you will have a much better idea of what your wedding will cost. You can then prioritize and allocate your money accordingly.

This budget is divided into fifteen categories: Ceremony, Wedding Attire, Photography, Videography, Stationery, Reception, Music, Bakery, Flowers, Decorations, Transportation, Rental Items, Gifts, Parties, and Miscellaneous.

At the beginning of each category is the percentage of a total wedding budget that is typically spent in that category. Multiply your intended wedding budget by this percent-

age and write that amount in the "Typically" space provided.

To determine the total cost of your wedding, estimate the amount of money you will spend on each item in the budget analysis and write that amount in the "Budget" column after each item. Items printed in italics are traditionally paid for by the groom or his family.

Add all the "Budget" amounts within each category and write the total amount in the "Subtotal" space at the end of each category. Then add all the "Subtotal" figures to come up with your final wedding budget. The "Actual" column is for you to input your actual expenses as you purchase items or hire your service providers. Writing down the actual expenses will help you stay within your budget.

If you find, after adding up all your "Subtotals," that the total amount is more than what you had in mind to spend, simply decide which items are more important to you and adjust your expenses accordingly.

When planning a wedding on a budget of $10,000 or less, you will need to remember some general tips:

• Prioritize! Sit down with your fiancé and decide what items are most important to you as a couple, what you and your guests will enjoy (or not miss) the most, where you want to splurge, what items a friend or family member can help provide, and what aspects you can possibly skip all together.

• Be up-front about your budget. Tell each vendor what you have budgeted for that aspect of the wedding and see if they will work within or close to that amount.

• Ask about specials, discounts and packaged deals. Some vendors will negotiate and some won't, but you will never know if you don't ask!

• Don't overdo the DIY projects. Make a list of materials and manpower for all craft and DIY projects to be sure you're even saving money. Then, create a realistic timeline and be sure to ask for help.

• Accept offers for help, big and small. Friends, family, coworkers and even acquaintances will offer their services, skills and assistance in every area from invitation design to putting together favors. Accept graciously; people love feeling included in your Big Day.

• Be picky about your guest list. Invite the most meaningful people in your life, and keep in mind, the smaller the guest list, the more options you'll have for your money. Easy places to trim are anyone you haven't seen personally in a few years, and people who made your guest list only because you were invited to their weddings.

## CEREMONY

- ❏ Ceremony Site Fee
- ❏ Officiant's Fee
- ❏ Officiant's Gratuity
- ❏ Guest Book/Pen/ Penholder
- ❏ Ring Bearer Pillow
- ❏ Flower Girl Basket

## WEDDING ATTIRE

- ❏ Bridal Gown
- ❏ Alterations
- ❏ Headpiece/Veil
- ❏ Gloves
- ❏ Jewelry
- ❏ Garter/Stockings
- ❏ Shoes
- ❏ Hairdresser
- ❏ Makeup Artist
- ❏ Manicure/Pedicure
- ❏ Groom's Formal Wear

## PHOTOGRAPHY

- ❏ Bride & Groom's Album
- ❏ Engagement Photograph
- ❏ Formal Bridal Portrait
- ❏ Parents' Album
- ❏ Proofs/Previews
- ❏ Digital Files
- ❏ Extra Prints

## VIDEOGRAPHY

- ❏ Main Video
- ❏ Titles
- ❏ Extra Hours
- ❏ Photo Montage
- ❏ Extra Copies

## STATIONERY

- ❏ Invitations
- ❏ Response Cards
- ❏ Reception Cards
- ❏ Ceremony Cards
- ❏ Pew Cards
- ❏ Seating/Place Cards
- ❏ Rain Cards
- ❏ Maps
- ❏ Ceremony Programs
- ❏ Announcements
- ❏ Thank-You Notes
- ❏ Stamps
- ❏ Calligraphy
- ❏ Napkins/ Matchbooks

## RECEPTION

- ❏ Reception Site Fee
- ❏ Hors d'Oeuvres
- ❏ Main Meal/Caterer
- ❏ Liquor/Beverages
- ❏ Bartending/Bar Setup Fee

## RECEPTION (cont)

- ❏ Corkage Fee
- ❏ Fee to Pour Coffee
- ❏ Service Providers' Meals
- ❏ Gratuity
- ❏ Party Favors
- ❏ Disposable Cameras
- ❏ Rose Petals/Rice
- ❏ Gift Attendant
- ❏ Parking Fee/Valet Services

## MUSIC

- ❏ Ceremony Music
- ❏ Reception Music

## BAKERY

- ❏ Wedding Cake
- ❏ Groom's Cake
- ❏ Cake Delivery/ Setup Fee
- ❏ Cake-Cutting Fee
- ❏ Cake Top
- ❏ Cake Knife/ Toasting Glasses

## FLOWERS

### Bouquets
- ❏ Bride
- ❏ Tossing

# CHECKLIST OF BUDGET ITEMS

## FLOWERS (cont)

❑ Maid of Honor
❑ Bridesmaid

### Floral Hairpieces
❑ Maid of Honor/
  Bridesmaids
❑ Flower Girl

### Corsages
❑ Bride's Going Away
❑ Family Members

### Boutonnieres
❑ Groom
❑ Ushers/Other
  Family Members

### Ceremony Site
❑ Main Altar
❑ Altar Candelabra
❑ Aisle Pews

### Reception Site
❑ Head Table
❑ Guest Tables
❑ Buffet Table
❑ Punch Table
❑ Cake Table
❑ Cake
❑ Cake Knife
❑ Toasting Glasses
❑ Floral Delivery/
  Setup Fee

## DECORATIONS

❑ Table Centerpieces
❑ Balloons

## TRANSPORTATION

❑ Transportation

## RENTAL ITEMS

❑ Bridal Slip
❑ Ceremony
  Accessories
❑ Tent/Canopy
❑ Dance Floor
❑ Tables/Chairs
❑ Linen/Tableware
❑ Heaters
❑ Lanterns
❑ Other Rental Items

## GIFTS

❑ Bride's Gift
❑ Groom's Gift
❑ Bridesmaids' Gifts
❑ Ushers' Gifts

## PARTIES

❑ Engagement Party
❑ Bachelor Party
❑ Bachelorette Party
❑ Bridesmaids'
  Luncheon
❑ Rehearsal Dinner
❑ Day-After Brunch

## MISCELLANEOUS

❑ Newspaper
  Announcements
❑ Marriage License
❑ Prenuptial
  Agreement
❑ Bridal Gown
  Preservation
❑ Bridal Bouquet
  Preservation
❑ Wedding
  Consultant
❑ Wedding Planning
  Online
❑ Taxes

| WEDDING BUDGET | Budget | Actual |
|---|---|---|
| **YOUR TOTAL WEDDING BUDGET** | $ | $ |
| **CEREMONY (Typically = 5% of Budget)** | $ | $ |
| Ceremony Site Fee | $ | $ |
| Officiant's Fee | $ | $ |
| Officiant's Gratuity | $ | $ |
| Guest Book/Pen/Penholder | $ | $ |
| Ring Bearer Pillow | $ | $ |
| Flower Girl Basket | $ | $ |
| **Subtotal 1** | $ | $ |

| WEDDING ATTIRE (Typically = 10% of Budget) | Budget | Actual |
|---|---|---|
| **WEDDING ATTIRE (Typically = 10% of Budget)** | $ | $ |
| Bridal Gown | $ | $ |
| Alterations | $ | $ |
| Headpiece/Veil | $ | $ |
| Gloves | $ | $ |
| Jewelry | $ | $ |
| Garter/Stockings | $ | $ |
| Shoes | $ | $ |
| Hairdresser | $ | $ |
| Makeup Artist | $ | $ |
| Manicure/Pedicure | $ | $ |
| Groom's Formal Wear | $ | $ |
| **Subtotal 2** | $ | $ |

| PHOTOGRAPHY (Typically = 9% of Budget) | Budget | Actual |
|---|---|---|
| **PHOTOGRAPHY (Typically = 9% of Budget)** | $ | $ |
| Bride & Groom's Album | $ | $ |
| Engagement Photograph | $ | $ |
| Formal Bridal Portrait | $ | $ |
| Parents' Album | $ | $ |
| Proofs/Previews | $ | $ |

## BUDGET ANALYSIS WORKSHEET

| WEDDING BUDGET | Budget | Actual |
|---|---|---|
| **PHOTOGRAPHY (CONT.)** | | |
| Digital Files | $ | $ |
| Extra Prints | $ | $ |
| **Subtotal 3** | $ | $ |

| | Budget | Actual |
|---|---|---|
| **VIDEOGRAPHY (Typically = 5% of Budget)** | $ | $ |
| Main Video | $ | $ |
| Titles | $ | $ |
| Extra Hours | $ | $ |
| Photo Montage | $ | $ |
| Extra Copies | $ | $ |
| **Subtotal 4** | $ | $ |

| | Budget | Actual |
|---|---|---|
| **STATIONERY (Typically = 4% of Budget)** | $ | $ |
| Invitations | $ | $ |
| Response Cards | $ | $ |
| Reception Cards | $ | $ |
| Ceremony Cards | $ | $ |
| Pew Cards | $ | $ |
| Seating/Place Cards | $ | $ |
| Rain Cards | $ | $ |
| Maps | $ | $ |
| Ceremony Programs | $ | $ |
| Announcements | $ | $ |
| Thank-You Notes | $ | $ |
| Stamps | $ | $ |
| Calligraphy | $ | $ |
| Napkins/Matchbooks | $ | $ |
| **Subtotal 5** | $ | $ |

| WEDDING BUDGET | Budget | Actual |
|---|---|---|
| **RECEPTION (Typically = 35% of Budget)** | $ | $ |
| Reception Site Fee | $ | $ |
| Hors d'Oeuvres | $ | $ |
| Main Meal/Caterer | $ | $ |
| Liquor/Beverages | $ | $ |
| Bartending/Bar Setup Fee | $ | $ |
| Corkage Fee | $ | $ |
| Fee to Pour Coffee | $ | $ |
| Service Providers' Meals | $ | $ |
| Gratuity | $ | $ |
| Party Favors | $ | $ |
| Disposable Cameras | $ | $ |
| Rose Petals/Rice | $ | $ |
| Gift Attendant | $ | $ |
| Parking Fee/Valet Services | $ | $ |
| **Subtotal 6** | $ | $ |

| MUSIC (Typically = 5% of Budget) | $ | $ |
|---|---|---|
| Ceremony Music | $ | $ |
| Reception Music | $ | $ |
| **Subtotal 7** | $ | $ |

| BAKERY (Typically = 2% of Budget) | $ | $ |
|---|---|---|
| Wedding Cake | $ | $ |
| Groom's Cake | $ | $ |
| Cake Delivery/Setup Fee | $ | $ |
| Cake-Cutting Fee | $ | $ |
| Cake Top | $ | $ |
| Cake Knife/Toasting Glasses | $ | $ |
| **Subtotal 8** | $ | $ |

## BUDGET ANALYSIS WORKSHEET

| WEDDING BUDGET | Budget | Actual |
|---|---|---|
| **FLOWERS (Typically = 6% of Budget)** | $ | $ |
| **Bouquets** | | |
| Bride | $ | $ |
| Tossing | $ | $ |
| Maid of Honor | $ | $ |
| Bridesmaids | $ | $ |
| **Floral Hairpieces** | | |
| Maid of Honor/Bridesmaids | $ | $ |
| Flower Girl | $ | $ |
| **Corsages** | | |
| Bride's Going Away | $ | $ |
| Family Members | $ | $ |
| **Boutonnieres** | | |
| Groom | $ | $ |
| Ushers/Other Family Members | $ | $ |
| **Ceremony Site** | | |
| Main Altar | $ | $ |
| Altar Candelabra | $ | $ |
| Aisle Pews | $ | $ |
| **Reception Site** | | |
| Reception Site | $ | $ |
| Head Table | $ | $ |
| Guest Tables | $ | $ |
| Buffet Table | $ | $ |
| Punch Table | $ | $ |
| Cake Table | $ | $ |
| Cake | $ | $ |
| Cake Knife | $ | $ |
| Toasting Glasses | $ | $ |
| Floral Delivery/Setup Fee | $ | $ |
| **Subtotal 9** | $ | $ |

| WEDDING BUDGET | Budget | Actual |
|---|---|---|
| **Decorations (Typically = 3% of Budget)** | $ | $ |
| Table Centerpieces | $ | $ |
| Balloons | $ | $ |
| **Subtotal 10** | $ | $ |

| TRANSPORTATION<br>**(Typically = 2% of Budget)** | $ | $ |
|---|---|---|
| Transportation | $ | $ |
| **Subtotal 11** | $ | $ |

| **RENTAL ITEMS (Typically = 3% of Budget)** | $ | $ |
|---|---|---|
| Bridal Slip | $ | $ |
| Ceremony Accessories | $ | $ |
| Tent/Canopy | $ | $ |
| Dance Floor | $ | $ |
| Tables/Chairs | $ | $ |
| Linen/Tableware | $ | $ |
| Heaters | $ | $ |
| Lanterns | $ | $ |
| Other Rental Items | $ | $ |
| **Subtotal 12** | $ | $ |

| **GIFTS (Typically = 3% of Budget)** | $ | $ |
|---|---|---|
| Bride's Gift | $ | $ |
| Groom's Gift | $ | $ |
| Bridesmaids' Gifts | $ | $ |
| Ushers' Gifts | $ | $ |
| **Subtotal 13** | $ | $ |

## BUDGET ANALYSIS WORKSHEET

| WEDDING BUDGET | Budget | Actual |
|---|---|---|
| **PARTIES (Typically = 4% of Budget)** | $ | $ |
| Engagement Party | $ | $ |
| Bridal Shower | $ | $ |
| Bachelor Party | $ | $ |
| Bachelorette Party | $ | $ |
| Bridesmaids' Luncheon | $ | $ |
| Rehearsal Dinner | $ | $ |
| **Subtotal 14** | $ | $ |

| | Budget | Actual |
|---|---|---|
| **MISCELLANEOUS (Typically = 4% of Budget)** | $ | $ |
| Newspaper Announcements | $ | $ |
| Marriage License | $ | $ |
| Prenuptial Agreement | $ | $ |
| Bridal Gown Preservation | $ | $ |
| Bridal Bouquet Preservation | $ | $ |
| Wedding Consultant | $ | $ |
| Wedding Planning Online | $ | $ |
| Taxes | $ | $ |
| **Subtotal 15** | $ | $ |

| | Budget | Actual |
|---|---|---|
| **GRAND TOTAL (Add "Budget" & "Actual" Subtotals 1-15)** | $ | $ |

# Wedding Consultant

WEDDING CONSULTANTS ARE PROFESSIONALS whose training, expertise, and contacts will help make your wedding as close to perfect as it can possibly be. They can save you considerable time, money, and stress when planning your wedding.

Contrary to what many people believe, a wedding consultant is part of your wedding budget, not an extra expense! Wedding consultants have information on many ceremony and reception sites as well as reliable service providers, which will save you hours of investigation and legwork.

**Options:** A consultant can help you plan the whole event from the beginning to the end, helping you formulate a budget, negotiating at vendor meetings, and helping you select your ceremony and reception site, flowers, invitations, and service providers.

Or, a wedding consultant can help you just at the end by coordinating the rehearsal and the wedding day. Remember, you want to feel like a guest at your own wedding. You and your family should not have to worry about any details on that special day. This is the wedding consultant's job!

**Things to Consider:** Wedding consultants can save you stress by ensuring that what you are planning is correct and that the service providers you hire are reliable and professional. Most service providers recommended by wedding consultants will go out of their way to do an excellent job for you so that the wedding consultant will continue to recommend their services.

Just beware that some wedding consultants do receive kickbacks or commissions for referring or recommending vendors. This is not only unethical, it means you may not be getting the best prices or best services. A professional planner or consultant should never accept "referral fees."

Additionally, ask how a wedding consultant charges, whether it's a package deal, per service on an à la carte basis, or per hour. Never hire a planner who tells you he or she charges based on the total final cost of your wedding. Get a complete breakdown in your contract of what the wedding planner will provide.

Price Range: $500 to $10,000

## Ideas to Save Money

▶ A good wedding consultant should be able to save you at least the amount of his or her fee by suggesting less expensive alternatives that still enhance your wedding or obtaining discounts from the service providers. If this is not enough, they are more than worth their fee by serving as an intermediary between you and your parents and vendors.

▶ Hire a day-of wedding consultant only. He or she can do anything from setting up flowers to setting tables to tying ribbons on ceremony programs. A day-of consultant helps keep vendors and the wedding party organized. Additionally, a consultant can take care of small mishaps throughout the day so the couple is never bothered and can fully enjoy their event.

▶ Ask an organized friend to act as your wedding coordinator. He or she can keep track of your vendors on the wedding day, help with setup, and much more.

▶ Many reception venues include a day-of wedding coordinator in their rental price. Find a venue who provides this helpful person.

▶ "We weren't sure about spending the money for a wedding consultant, but she ended up being a life-saver. When our florist completely mixed up our order and delivered flowers that looked nothing like the samples I'd OK'd, our consultant not only made sure they brought us the correct bouquets, but she got us some of our money back after the wedding."
~ Tori G., Naples, FL

▶ "Instead of hiring a wedding planner, I contacted the New Orleans Convention & Visitors Bureau, and they had great (free!) recommendations for venues, caterers, and things to do for my out-of-town guests."
~ Stacy K., Lafayette, LA

## WEDDING CONSULTANT COMPARISON CHART

| Questions | POSSIBILITY 1 |
|---|---|
| What is the name and address of the wedding consultant business? | |
| What is the website. phone number and e-mail of the wedding consultant? | |
| What is the name and phone number of my contact person? | |
| How many years of professional experience do you have? | |
| How many consultants are in your company? | |
| Are you a member of the Association of Bridal Consultants? | |
| What services can you provide? | |
| What are your hourly fees? | |
| What is your fee for complete wedding planning? | |
| What is your fee to oversee the rehearsal and wedding day? | |
| What vendors do you have good relationships with that can save me money? | |
| Do you receive commissions or referral fees from vendors? | |
| Will you attend vendor meetings with me? | |
| Can you describe a problem you encountered at a wedding and how you handled it? | |
| How will you dress on my wedding day? | |
| What is your payment policy? | |
| What is your cancellation policy? | |

| POSSIBILITY 2 | POSSIBILITY 3 |
|---|---|
| | |
| | |
| | |
| | |
| | |
| | |
| | |
| | |
| | |
| | |
| | |
| | |
| | |
| | |
| | |
| | |

# WEDDING CONSULTANT'S INFORMATION FORM

*Make a copy of this form and give it to your wedding consultant.*

## THE WEDDING OF:

Ceremony Site: _____ Phone Number: _____

Ceremony Address: _____

Reception Site: _____ Phone Number: _____

Reception Address: _____

| Ceremony Services | Contact Person | Arrival Time | Departure Time | Phone Number |
|---|---|---|---|---|
| Florist | | | | |
| Musicians | | | | |
| Officiant | | | | |
| Photographer | | | | |
| Rental Supplier | | | | |
| Site Coordinator | | | | |
| Soloist | | | | |
| Transportation | | | | |
| Videographer | | | | |

| Reception Services | Contact Person | Arrival Time | Departure Time | Phone Number |
|---|---|---|---|---|
| Baker | | | | |
| Bartender | | | | |
| Caterer | | | | |
| Florist | | | | |
| Gift Attendant | | | | |
| Guest Book Attendant | | | | |
| Musicians | | | | |
| Rental Supplier | | | | |
| Site Coordinator | | | | |
| Transportation | | | | |
| Valet Service | | | | |

# Jes & Caleb

Total Spent: $3,700

March 27, 2010 • Lancaster, Pennsylvania • 65 guests

Photography by Carissa of For You Love Me, www.foryouloveme.com

## Budget Breakdown

| | | | | |
|---|---|---|---|---|
| Attire | $580 | | Bar | $170 |
| Stationery | $50 | | Music | $50 |
| Ceremony & Reception Site | $1,045 | | Bakery | $160 |
| | | | Flowers | $0 |
| Photography | $0 | | Décor & Rental Items | $570 |
| Videography | N/A | | Miscellaneous | $635 |
| Food | $440 | | **Total** | **$3,700** |

**It's hard to believe that Jes and Caleb** planned their sweet vintage-minimalist wedding in less than 3 months! But, by creating a wedding planning game plan, using their creative talents, and relying on the help of family and friends, they were able to plan a beautiful wedding in a short timeframe *and* stick to their small budget. Jes and Caleb had a blast making music playlists and DIYing everything from paper flowers to coloring books for young guests. Says Jes, "Some days it got hectic and stressful, sure, but we tried to keep the real goal in mind: an awesome marriage, not a perfect wedding. Thankfully, we got both. ... I could go on forever. Our wedding was so much fun."

## FROM THE BRIDE

Caleb and I planned our wedding in a little under 3 months. And in the last week, we literally had nothing to do but wait for the big day. Don't think that because you have to cut costs in a certain area that it has to come off looking cheap. Keeping things really simple means making it elegant. Your guest don't care about a 4-course dinner, they care about *you*. They love weddings that bring them into the relationship. Give them one awesome course, a glass of wine, and then put all the money you've saved after that into whatever is most important to you and your fiancé. Show off who you are as a couple. If you start being too concerned with the guests and what they think, you'll lose yourselves in the process.

## CEREMONY

Our main plan was to have our friends and family sitting at their dinner tables during the ceremony so it would be intimate and they could drink iced tea while they watched us get married. Once we saw Progressive Galleries, the search for a venue was over. It was a high rental — 1/4 of our total budget — but it fit our style and purposes perfectly.

## BAKERY

We also splurged on dessert. We live in Philly and my favorite cupcakes are from Flying Monkey in the Reading Terminal Market. They were a must-have.

## STATIONERY

We saved on everything else! We bought invitations from Target and incorporated our engagement photos in a train museum, taken by Caleb's sister. They came to $50, including stamps!

## PHOTOGRAPHY

The folks at For You Love Me are great friends who gave us an awesome deal!

## FOOD

We figured out a dinner that was elegant but cheap and could be done with very little prep: a cheese board, cocktail shrimp, corn muffins, meatballs, crudites with hummus, and quiche. We asked our moms to each bake a batch of cookies for dessert.

## DÉCOR & FLOWERS

Caleb and I DIYed everything we could (it helps a lot that Caleb is an amazing designer). This included our escort chart, table markers, programs, favors, invitations, and kid-favors, which were little coloring books. We recruited friends for a day of paper-flower making, which meant a huge savings. We collected little jars from our kitchens and from thrift stores to use for candles and large mason jars for centerpieces that we filled with gathered twigs and paper flowers. We borrowed things from our moms and their friends. We asked people from Caleb's parents' church to help serve the tables. We found two bolts of really nice fabric at a discount department store for $1 a yard and cut the fabric into table cloths.

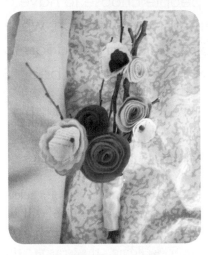

## MUSIC

For music, we made playlists and played them through our computer.

## ADVICE

My best advice is just ask for help! What I have learned the most through our wedding is that people love weddings. They love to be a part. Appeal to the older women in your families. They have serving platters they'd love to loan you; they have time to help you DIY favors and centerpieces. Get your friends to bake or cut celery and carrots for the appetizers. If you can delegate graciously, you'll find you have more people who want to help you than you even need!

# Ceremony

YOUR CEREMONY IS A REFLECTION OF who you are. It can be as simple or as elaborate as fits within your budget. Many people choose to have a traditional ceremony in a church, while others take their special day outdoors to a park or the beach.

## CEREMONY SITE FEE

The ceremony site fee is the fee to rent a facility for your wedding. In churches, cathedrals, chapels, temples, or synagogues, this fee may include the organist, wedding coordinator, custodian, changing rooms for the bridal party, and miscellaneous items such as kneeling cushions, aisle runner, and candelabra. Be sure to ask what the site fee includes prior to booking a facility.

Options: Churches, cathedrals, chapels, temples, synagogues, private homes, gardens, hotels, clubs, halls, parks, museums, yachts, wineries, and beaches.

Things to Consider: Your selection of a ceremony site will be influenced by the formality of your wedding, the season, the number of guests expected, and your religious affiliation.

Make sure you ask about restrictions or guidelines regarding photography, videography, music, decorations, candles, and rice or rose petal-tossing.

Consider issues such as proximity of the ceremony site to the reception site, parking availability, handicapped accessibility, and time constraints.

Price Range: $100 - $1,000

## Ideas to Save Money

▶ Have your ceremony at the same facility as your reception to save a second rental fee.

▶ Saturdays are the most popular days for weddings, so choose a Friday or Sunday. You can usually save at least $200 or more.

▶ Have your ceremony at a state park or beach, which typically only charge a very small fee. Inquire about parking, bathrooms and seating restrictions.

▶ At a church or temple, ask if there is another wedding that day and share the cost of floral decorations, a chuppah, or altar arrangements with that bride.

▶ Membership in a church, temple, or club can reduce rental fees. Also, members at these venues typically get first pick of dates and times for weddings.

▶ At an intimate garden or beach wedding, have guests stand and omit the cost of renting chairs.

## Real Couples' Weddings

▶ "My husband and I wanted to get married in a beautiful church in New York City, but we were told because we were not members, we would have to make a hefty donation to the church. We then found out that the only time available for our ceremony would be 10 a.m. How could we have a 10 a.m. ceremony and a sit-down dinner reception at 6 p.m.? After some back and forth, we learned that the good time slots are reserved for church members who attend weekly services. We ended up booking a less formal venue, which wasn't our original vision, but it did save us about $1,500 and allowed us to get the Saturday afternoon ceremony time we wanted."
~ Valerie K., Patterson, NJ

▶ "We were married in Greenwell State Park in Maryland. They have an English rose garden that was so incredibly beautiful as the backdrop for our ceremony, and also saved us a bundle on buying or renting any flowers or decorations. You'll probably have to jazz up a church, but getting married outside in a beautiful location means less stress, no setup, and saving money."
~ Sarah P., Bethesda, MD

▶ "We wanted a beach ceremony and hired a videographer to record it. Not only was it difficult to hear anything over the sound of waves crashing, but there were strangers and beachgoers milling around and stopping to stare during the ceremony. Plus, you may need to rent chairs for your guests, so that's an added expense. A wedding on the beach sounds romantic and simple, but it can be anything but!"
~ Heidi M., Tucson, AZ

## OFFICIANT'S FEE

The officiant's fee is the fee paid to the person who performs your wedding ceremony.

**Options:** Priest, Clergyman, Minister, Pastor, Chaplain, Rabbi, Judge, Justice of the Peace, or loved one

**Things to Consider:** Some officiants may not accept a fee, depending on your relationship with him or her. If a fee is refused, send a donation to the officiant's church or synagogue. Discuss with your officiant the readings you would like incorporated into your ceremony.

**Price Range:** $30 - $500

### Ideas to Save Money

▶ Have a friend or family member become ordained to perform your ceremony. Simple and inexpensive online programs ($30 and up) are available in every state. Prices and guidelines vary.

▶ Ask your family's long-time pastor or rabbi to perform the service for you. Someone who knows you well will probably waive his or her fee.

▶ "I wanted to include my best guy friend in my wedding, but I didn't like the idea of a 'bridesman,' so we paid $40 for him to become ordained to marry us. We wrote a ceremony script for him and he incorporated a few bits and pieces about how we met (he was there) and fell in love. It was truly special — so much more so than hiring an expensive officiant who we didn't know and didn't know us."
~ Kim & Daniel K., Bowling Green, OH

## OFFICIANT'S GRATUITY

The officiant's gratuity is a discretionary amount of money given to the officiant.

**Things to Consider:** The groom puts this fee in a sealed envelope and gives it to his best man or wedding consultant, who gives it to the officiant either before or immediately after the ceremony.

**Price Range:** $50 - $250

▶ The officiant's gratuity should depend on your relationship with the officiant and the amount of time he or she has spent with you prior to the ceremony. If he or she is someone you only know briefly, you do not need to leave a large amount of gratuity.

## GUEST BOOK/PEN/PENHOLDER

The guest book is a formal register that your guests sign as they arrive at the ceremony or reception. It serves as a memento of who attended your wedding. This book is often placed outside the ceremony or reception site, along with a nice pen and penholder. A guest book attendant is responsible for inviting all guests to sign in. A younger sibling or close friend who is not part of the wedding party may be well-suited for this position.

**Options:** Traditionally, couples will have a professional book with photos of the them and space for guests to write a short note or a large photo with space to write around the border.

**Things to Consider:** If you are planning a large ceremony, consider having more than one pen so that your guests don't have to wait in line to sign in.

**Price Range:** $10 - $100

### Ideas to Save Money

▶ Build a wish tree out of a small sapling or potted plant. Cut large leaves out of construction paper and have your guests write a note on them and tie them to the branches of the tree with ribbon. Plant the tree after the wedding.

▶ Have guests write a note and drop it inside a birdcage. Birdcages can be found at antique stores, thrift stores, eBay, or other online retailers.

▶ A typewriter, bought from a flea market or antique store, can serve as a fun, unique and inexpensive guest book. Just provide a stack of sheets of paper or a long scroll of paper and have guests type notes as they enter your ceremony or reception.

## RING BEARER PILLOW OR RING DISH

The ring bearer, usually a boy between the ages of 4 and 8, carries the bride and groom's rings or mock rings on a pillow or in a small dish. He follows the maid of honor and precedes the flower girl or bride in the processional.

**Options:** Ring pillows and ring dishes come in many styles and colors. You can find them at most gift shops, bridal boutiques and online wedding retailers.

**Things to Consider:** If the ring bearer is very young (less than 7 years), place mock rings on the pillow in place of the real rings to prevent losing them. If mock rings are used, instruct your ring bearer to put the pillow upside down during the recessional so your guests don't see them.

**Price Range:** $15 - $75

▶ Make your own ring bearer pillow. Take a small pillow and sew a pretty ribbon to it to hold the rings.

▶ Sew your own ring pillow. Simple instructions can be found online. Choose the fabric/s and ribbon that match your wedding colors and theme.

▶ Use something meaningful to you as a ring dish to avoid purchasing one. A large seashell, beautiful bowl, or jewelry box could all hold rings.

**Real Couples' Weddings**

▶ "My young son and nephew were the ring bearers for our beach wedding, and I could just see the rings falling into the sand and being lost forever. I gave them each a small, hinged box that we found for only $3 apiece at Ross, which looked nice and kept the rings safe and sound."
~ Jessica B., Coral Gables, FL

## FLOWER GIRL BASKET

The flower girl, usually between the ages of 4 and 8, carries a basket filled with flowers, rose petals, or paper rose petals to scatter as she walks down the aisle. She follows the ring bearer or maid of honor and precedes the bride during the processional.

**Options:** Flower girl baskets come in many styles and colors. You can find them at most florists, gift shops, and bridal boutiques.

**Things to Consider:** Discuss any restrictions regarding rose petals, flowers, or paper-tossing with your ceremony site.

Select a basket that complements your ring bearer pillow. If the flower girl is very young (less than 7 years), consider giving her a small bouquet instead of a flower basket.

**Price Range:** $5 - $75

▶ Buy an inexpensive basket at a crafts store and decorate it with silk flowers or a ribbon.

▶ Ask your florist if you can borrow a basket and attach a pretty bow to it.

**Real Couples' Weddings**

▶ "We bought an inexpensive little girl's purse and gave it to the flower girl to use during the ceremony and keep as a gift. What little girl doesn't like a present?"

~ Kate F., Arlington, TX

# CEREMONY SITE COMPARISON CHART

| Questions | POSSIBILITY 1 |
|---|---|
| What is the name and address of the ceremony site? | |
| What is the website and e-mail of the ceremony site? | |
| What is the name and phone number of my contact person? | |
| What dates and times are available? | |
| What is the ceremony site fee? | |
| What is the payment/cancellation policy? | |
| Do vows need to be approved? | |
| Does the facility have liability insurance? | |
| What are the minimum/maximum number of guests allowed? | |
| What restrictions are there with regards to religion? | |
| Is an officiant available? At what cost? | |
| Are outside officiants allowed? | |
| What music restrictions are there, if any? | |
| What photography restrictions are there, if any? | |
| What videography restrictions are there, if any? | |
| What floral decorations are available/ allowed? | |
| How many parking spaces are available for my wedding party and guests? | |

| POSSIBILITY 2 | POSSIBILITY 3 |
|---|---|
|  |  |
|  |  |
|  |  |
|  |  |
|  |  |
|  |  |
|  |  |
|  |  |
|  |  |
|  |  |
|  |  |
|  |  |
|  |  |
|  |  |
|  |  |
|  |  |

## PEW SEATING ARRANGEMENTS

*Be sure to designate seating arrangements for the bride's family section and groom's family section.*

- **Pew** _____

_____

_____

_____

_____

_____

- **Pew** _____

_____

_____

_____

_____

_____

- **Pew** _____

_____

_____

_____

_____

_____

- **Pew** _____

_____

_____

_____

_____

_____

_____

- **Pew** _____

_____

_____

_____

_____

_____

_____

- **Pew** _____

_____

_____

_____

_____

_____

_____

- **Pew** _____

_____

_____

_____

_____

_____

_____

- **Pew** _____

_____

_____

_____

_____

_____

_____

- **Pew** _____

_____

_____

_____

_____

_____

_____

**Bride's Vows:**

_____

_____

_____

_____

_____

_____

_____

_____

**Groom's Vows:**

_____

_____

_____

_____

_____

_____

_____

_____

**Personalized Ring Ceremony:**

_____

_____

_____

_____

_____

_____

_____

## CEREMONY READING SELECTIONS

| SOURCE | Selection | Read By | When |
|--------|-----------|---------|------|
|  |  |  |  |
|  |  |  |  |
|  |  |  |  |
|  |  |  |  |
|  |  |  |  |
|  |  |  |  |
|  |  |  |  |
|  |  |  |  |
|  |  |  |  |
|  |  |  |  |
|  |  |  |  |
|  |  |  |  |
|  |  |  |  |
|  |  |  |  |
|  |  |  |  |
|  |  |  |  |
|  |  |  |  |
|  |  |  |  |

# Attire & Beauty

BRIDAL GOWNS COME IN A WIDE VARIETY of styles, materials, colors, lengths, and prices. You should order your gown at least four to six months before your wedding if your gown has to be made and then fitted.

## BRIDAL GOWN

In selecting your gown, keep in mind the time of year and formality of your wedding. It is a good idea to look at bridal magazines to compare the various styles and colors. If you see a gown you like, call boutiques in your area to see if they carry that line. If you can, always try on a gown before ordering it. If ordering from an online retailer, it is smart to order more than one size to avoid paying for shipping and handling multiple times.

Options: Different gown styles complement different body types. Here are some general tips when choosing your dress, although you should wear what makes you feel beautiful and special:

- A short, heavy figure: To look taller and slimmer, avoid knit fabrics. Use the princess or A-line style. Chiffon is the best fabric choice because it produces a floating effect although a short bride can get lost in a ballgown. A sturdy fabric like silk shantung or taffeta can hide weight as well.

- A short, thin figure: An empire or natural waist style with bouffant skirt or classic sheath will produce a taller, more rounded figure. Chiffon and lace are good fabric choices.

- **A tall, heavy figure:** Princess or A-line styles are best for slimming the figure. Avoid clingy fabrics and note that an empire waist may draw attention to a big bust. Chiffon and lace fabrics are recommended.

- **A tall, thin figure:** Tiers, runching or flounces will help reduce the impression of height. A simple silhouette will look elegant; just be sure sleeves and hems are the right length. Satin, silk and lace are the best fabrics.

**Things to Consider:** In selecting your bridal gown, keep in mind the time of year and formality of your wedding. Look at bridal magazines and real weddings to compare various styles and shades, but don't be afraid to explore less traditional gowns, if you like.

When trying on gowns at a bridal salon, call and make an appointment before stopping in. Be aware that Saturdays are going to be the most popular shopping days. Bring your mother, sister, maid of honor, or mother-in-law along with you. Also bring something to tie your hair back with, a strapless bra, and a shoe with a heel about the height of what you will wear on your Big Day. It is also helpful to bring in tearsheets from magazines so you can show the boutique staff what you have in mind for your gown. Bring a digital camera and have someone take pictures of you in each dress from different angles, if the boutique allows it (some designers won't allow photos so their styles aren't copied).

When ordering a gown, make sure you order the correct size. If you are between sizes, order the larger one. You can always have your gown tailored down to fit, but it is not always possible to have it enlarged or to lose enough weight to fit into it! Don't forget to ask when your gown will arrive, and be sure to get this in writing. The gown should arrive at least six weeks before the wedding so you can have it tailored and select the appropriate accessories to complement it.

Be aware that some gown manufacturers will suggest ordering a size larger than needed. This requires more alterations, which may mean extra charges. Also, gowns often fail to arrive on time, creating unnecessary stress for you. Be sure to order your gown with enough time to allow for delivery delays and also be sure to check the reputation of the boutique before buying.

Price Range: $200 - $10,000

▶ Buy a secondhand dress. Shop for gently used or never-worn wedding gowns on sites like OnceWed.com and PreOwnedWeddingDresses. com. Just be sure to ask for details (has it been cleaned, staining, any minor tears, alterations from original design?) and get lots of good photos from every angle. If you can, find a dress near your area so you can see it and try it on in person.

▶ Ask about discontinued styles and watch for clearances and sample sales. Just be sure to check that older gowns and floor sample gowns have been cleaned, or else you'll need to pay for a cleaning.

▶ Instead of buying a custom gown, buy your gown "off the rack" from a retailer other than a bridal boutique. J. Crew, Ann Taylor, Nicole Miller and others offer beautiful wedding gowns for much lower prices than classic bridal brands. Consider buying a simple, classic style and embellishing it with a belt, necklace, or headpiece.

▶ Have a seamstress copy a style you love. If a designer gown is out of your budget, take the design to a seamstress you trust to have it copied. Get several swatches of different fabrics to find the perfect one. Research your seamstress thoroughly, ask other brides who they used for their handmade gowns, and be sure to give yourself at least 6 months for the sewing and fittings.

▶ Rent a gown, which usually costs about 40 to 60 percent of its retail price. Consider this practical option if you are not planning to preserve the gown. The disadvantage of renting, however, is that your options are more limited, and a rented gown usually does not fit as well as a custom-tailored gown.

▶ Know what makes one gown more expensive than another. Hand-beading will cost more than detailing done with a machine or glued on. Polyester and other synthetic fabrics will be cheaper than real silk. Check if seams lie flat, that buttons are sewn on tightly, and whether threads show through the seams. All these factors can determine the cost of a bridal gown, and note that the priciest designer gown isn't always the best quality.

▶ Shopping at a bridal boutique? Don't fall for the "upsell." When you tell the boutique salesperson your budget, it is completely common for her to pull gowns for you to try on that are slightly or sometimes *much* higher than what you have budgeted. Check on the price of the dresses before you put them on to avoid falling for something out of your price range.

▶ Restore or refurbish a family heirloom gown. Update the detailing, shorten the hem to make it more modern, or add your own personal touches.

▶ Wear a dress that's not a "wedding dress." Look for evening dresses from designers such as BCBG, Nicole Miller, Vera Wang, or ABS, in their non-wedding lines. You will often find gorgeous white, off-white and colored gowns with beautiful detailing, lace, and beading that are less than $500 simply because they aren't technically considered "wedding gowns."

## Real Couples' Weddings

▶ "Always pay for things for your wedding on your credit card, including your gown. I put $500 down for my dress when I ordered it, and a few months later, the bridal store closed. My credit card company helped me get my money back, thank goodness. If I had paid any other way, I know I would never have seen that money. Remember, you're putting thousands in deposits on things like photography, catering, the gown, etc. and you want to be protected in case a store or company disappears without warning."
~ Marianne T., Asheville, NC

## ALTERATIONS

Alterations may be necessary to make your gown fit perfectly. You may also want to consider making some modifications to your gown, such as shortening or lengthening the train, customizing the neckline, adding beading, adding a bustle, and so forth. Ask your bridal boutique what they charge for modifications.

Things to Consider: Alterations usually require several fittings. Allow four to six weeks for alterations to be completed. However, do not alter your gown months before the wedding or plan to lose a lot of weight right before the wedding, or you risk the gown not fitting properly.

Price Range: $50 - $500

## Ideas to Save Money

▶ If you have a lot of alterations to be done, find a bridal boutique that will provide alterations for your wedding gown and bridesmaids' dresses for a flat fee per dress.

▶ Many boutiques offer tailoring services, but you will often find a much better price by finding an independent tailor specializing in bridal gown alterations. Contact a few tailors in your area and ask for alteration pricing in advance.

▶ Avoid "rush" fees by having major alterations done several months out. Inquire about the price of alterations and the timeframe needed for them to avoid extra charges.

▶ An intricate gown can cost hundreds of dollars for extensive alterations. Some boutiques also charge more for alterations on "couture" gowns, simply because the original price was higher. A more simple gown will be much easier to have hemmed, bustled, taken in, etc., saving you a lot of money.

▶ If the changes are more simple, do your own alterations or ask a family member who is handy with a needle and thread to help you.

## Real Couples' Weddings

▶ "A great tailor is an invaluable money- and stress-saving resource for your gown, as well as your bridesmaids' dresses. Do lots of research — ask friends who've been recently married, visit forums online, or read other brides' feedback on Yelp.com and CitySearch.com."
~ Ann D., San Francisco, CA

## HEADPIECE/VEIL

The headpiece is the part of the bride's outfit to which the veil is attached.

**Options for Headpieces:** Bow, Garden Hat, Headband, Juliet Cap, Mantilla, Pillbox, Pouf, Tiara, Flower

**Options for Veils:** Ballet, Bird Cage, Blusher, Cathedral Length, Chapel Length, Fingertip, Flyaway

**Things to Consider:** You may want to wear a veil for the ceremony and remove it for the reception. If you do so, you can wear a different hairpiece for the reception.

Select a veil length that complements the formality of your dress and your event. For instance, a Cathedral or Chapel Length veil is appropriate for a formal wedding, but will be too dressy for an outdoor wedding; thus, choose a shorter veil like a Fingertip or Blusher. A Bird Cage veil is perfect for a vintage-style gown.

Consider the overall look you're trying to achieve with your gown, headpiece, veil, and hairstyle. If possible, schedule your hair test appointment for the day you go veil shopping so you can see how they coordinate.

**Price Range:** $5 - $500

### Ideas to Save Money

▶ Some boutiques offer a free headpiece or veil with the purchase of a gown. Make sure you ask for this before purchasing your gown.

▶ Have your florist provide a few extra stems of your main flower for your hair. The best long-lasting blooms include orchids, gardenias, daisies and roses. Avoid tulips or sweet peas or other flowers that wilt quickly.

▶ DIY your own headpiece for just a few dollars! Hot glue a silk flower or real flower (choose a hardy bloom like a gardenia) to a plastic comb or hairpin. You can also make a beautiful headband out of a piece of ribbon, a couple of hairpins, and sequins or beads. All you need is a needle and thread!

- Search online or on crafts sites like Etsy for handmade veils for less than you will probably pay at a bridal boutique.

- An inexpensive way to dress up your wedding-day hairstyle is with satin or grosgrain ribbon. Twist a piece of ribbon through an updo and pin with bobby pins, or wind a satin ribbon into a braid.

## Real Couples' Weddings

- "I had a laid-back rustic wedding, so I skipped wearing a veil all together, saving me at least $100. It just wasn't my style or my wedding day's style!"
~ Rachel O., Lexington, KY

## GLOVES

Gloves add a glamorous touch to a sleeveless gown for a more formal evening or a cold-weather wedding.

**Options:** Gloves come in various styles and lengths. Depending on the length of your sleeves, select gloves that reach above your elbow, just below your elbow, halfway between your wrist and elbow, or only to your wrist.

**Things to Consider:** You should not wear gloves if your gown has sleeves, in very warm weather, or if you're planning a small, informal wedding.

**Price Range:** $5 - $100

## Ideas to Save Money

- Shop vintage, secondhand and even costume stores for gloves. You can find them for just a few dollars!

## JEWELRY

Jewelry can beautifully accent your dress and be the perfect finishing touch.

**Options:** Pearls, multi-tiered necklace, bracelet, cuff, stud earrings, drop earrings with an updo, cocktail ring

**Things to Consider:** Brides look best with just a few pieces of jewelry. Select pieces of jewelry that can be classified as "something old, something new, something borrowed, or something blue."

Purchase complementary jewelry for your bridesmaids, to match the colors of their dresses. This will give your bridal party a coordinated look.

**Price Range:** $20 - $2,000

## Ideas to Save Money

▶ Rent high-end jewelry. For instance, a diamond necklace and earrings that cost thousands of dollars may rent for as little as $75 for a week. There are several reputable websites that offer this service and let you browse a wide selection of necklaces, earrings, bracelets and more.

▶ Shop for vintage jewelry online, at estate sales, and in antique stores.

▶ Borrow a piece of jewelry from a loved one for your Big Day. This can serve as your "something borrowed."

▶ If you're not picky about wearing real stones, you can find beautiful pieces that use fake stones or cubic zirconia in place of diamonds.

## GARTER

It is customary for the bride to wear a garter just above the knee on her wedding day. After the bouquet tossing ceremony, the groom takes the garter off the bride's leg. All the single men gather on the dance floor. The groom then tosses the garter to them over his back. According to age-old tradition, whoever catches the garter is the next to be married!

**Things to Consider:** You will need to choose the proper music for the garter toss. If you want to save your garter as a memento, wear a cheap one for the garter toss.

**Price Range:** $5 - $60

▶ Buy a garter set from a craft site like Etsy.com, which will cost less than purchasing one from a bridal boutique.

▶ Skip the garter toss tradition if it's not for you! Some brides find it antiquated and would rather not interrupt their reception.

**Real Couples' Weddings**

▶ "I made my own garter, which is just a few dollars worth of fabric, elastic and some ribbon. Look for online tutorials and DIY this simple project!"
~ Lacey G., Bentonville, AK

## SHOES

Options: Ballet flats, wedges, stilettos, sandals, slingbacks, cowboy boots

Things to Consider: Don't forget to break in your shoes well before your wedding day. Tight shoes can make you miserable!

Consider that you'll want shoes without a heel, such as wedges or flats, for an outdoor wedding on sand or grass so heels don't sink in or get dirty.

Price Range: $20 - $500

**Ideas to Save Money**

▶ Skip oddly hued shoes or all-white shoes (which aren't as wearable or long-lasting) and buy a great pair of metallic heels that you'll be able to wear again and again after the wedding.

▶ Shop designer shoe outlets and factory stores for deep discounts.

▶ Shop at the end of a season and find great sales. For instance, buy a pair of shoes on sale at the end of the summer and wear them the following spring or summer.

- ► If shoes aren't especially important to you, wear a pair you already own that will look nice in photos.

- ► "I had my eye on a pair of heels that were pretty pricey, so I signed up for Piperlime.com and Zappos.com's weekly emails and waited until I got one of their 'one day only, 25 percent off' emails to buy my shoes. Every $30 or $40 you can save adds up."
  ~ Meghan B., Kansas City, MO

## BRIDESMAIDS' DRESSES

Traditionally, the women in the wedding party all wear the same dress for a uniform look at the altar. Modernly, bridesmaids' dresses can be anything you choose — they can be the same color in different styles or even different dresses of different colors. Some brides even allow their bridesmaids to choose their own dresses by giving them color and skirt length guidelines.

**Things to Consider:** Consider the time of day, year and formality of your wedding when choosing bridesmaids' dresses. Long dresses or tea-length dresses may be best for formal weddings, whereas short dresses may be more appropriate for an informal wedding. Also, consider the temperature as certain fabrics will be better for hot or humid weather than others.

If your bridesmaids are a wide variety of shapes and sizes, you may want to consider allowing them to buy the style of dress that fits their bodies the best, from the same retailer and in the same color.

Bridesmaids' dresses can be purchased just about anywhere — from bridal salons to department stores to online retailers. Bridesmaids should get their dresses two to four months before the wedding to account for shipping times and alterations.

Beware that bridesmaids' dresses from traditional bridal retailers tend to run big in size — a size 6 girl may wear a size 10 bridesmaids' dress. And, it is not uncommon for a store to order dresses that are much too large in hopes of charging more for expensive alterations. If you're concerned about the unconventional sizes of bridesmaids' dresses, stick with off-the-rack dresses that the wedding party can either try on in person or exchange through the mail if the fit is off.

Price Range: $25 - $450

## Ideas to Save Money

▶ Dresses from bridal boutiques will generally be more expensive, so shop at nontraditional retailers, such as mall and online stores. Popular resources include J.Crew, Anthropologie, Ann Taylor Loft, ModCloth. com, VictoriasSecret.com, Forever 21, department stores, and more. Another big plus is that dresses from these stores are returnable or exchangeable, whereas dresses from bridal stores are not.

## Real Couples' Weddings

▶ "I ordered chocolate brown silk dresses for my bridesmaids, and when they arrived, they were definitely a polyester-blend satin and not silk. The material looked cheap and puckered after alterations. Plus, two of the 'invisible zippers' broke. I could not believe how shoddy the material and cratfsmanship was on a $200 dress. In retrospect, it would have been better to buy dresses I could see and feel in person."
~ Katie A., Saddle River, NJ

▶ "I was the only member of the wedding party for my friend's small, beach wedding. She was sweet enough to tell me I could buy any dress I wanted, as long as it was light purple, in fitting with her color scheme. I'm not kidding when I say I found the perfect, flowy dress on clearance for $9.99! I was so grateful not to have to spend $300!"
~ Paige S., Seattle, WA

▶ "I didn't think it was fair to have a wedding on a small budget but make my wedding party spend a lot of money on their dresses. For my evening wedding, I asked them all to wear a black cocktail dress (something most people already have). Every dress was different, but they all looked great."
~ Claire M., Dayton, OH

## HAIRDRESSER

Many brides prefer to have their hair professionally arranged with their headpiece the day of the wedding rather than trying to do it themselves.

Things to Consider: Have your professional hairdresser experiment with your hair and headpiece before your wedding day so there are no surprises. Most hairdressers will include the cost of a trial session in your package. They will try several styles on you and write down the specifics of each one so that things go quickly and smoothly on your wedding day.

Bring tearsheets from magazines so you can give your hairdresser an idea of what you want. On the big day, you can go to the salon or have the stylist meet you at your home or dressing site.

Price Range: $0 - $200

### Ideas to Save Money

▶ Negotiate having your hair done free of charge or at a discount in exchange for bringing your mother, your fiancé's mother, and your bridal party to the salon.

▶ Contact a local beauty school where a student will create your hairstyle under the watchful eye of an instructor, for a very discounted price. Just don't get a haircut or color treatment close to your wedding date, in case it doesn't come out to your liking.

▶ Have a friend do your hair in lieu of giving you a wedding gift, just be sure to do a trial run ahead of time so you can determine the best style and technique.

### Real Couples' Weddings

▶ "When you book an appointment at a hair salon, ask for an updo for a 'formal event' instead of a wedding, and you'll save off the much more expensive bridal package price."
~ Jaimie K., Denver, CO

## MAKEUP ARTIST

A professional makeup artist will apply makeup that should last throughout the day and will often provide you with samples for touch-ups. Be sure to have your wedding-day hair done first.

**Things to Consider:** You can either go to the salon or have the makeup artist meet you at your home or dressing site. In selecting a makeup artist, make sure he or she has been trained in makeup for photography. It is very important to wear the proper amount of makeup for photographs. One of the perks of using a professional is he or she will have access to special products, such as airbrush foundation, which will make skin look flawless on camera.

When you use a makeup artist, bring your own mascara and lipstick, as those products shouldn't be reused from client to client.

Price Range:  $0 - $150

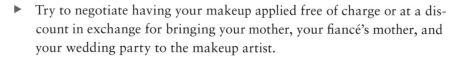

### Ideas to Save Money

▶ Try to negotiate having your makeup applied free of charge or at a discount in exchange for bringing your mother, your fiancé's mother, and your wedding party to the makeup artist.

▶ Ask a trusted friend to apply your makeup, just be sure to do a test run and supply the products you want to use.

▶ Go to a high-end makeup counter or store and have them apply your makeup. The only cost to you is purchasing the makeup products you'll want to use for touchups or in the future. Just be sure to have a trial run before the big day and be specific about the look you want.

### Real Couples' Weddings

▶ "Paying for 6 bridesmaids to have their makeup professionally done wasn't in my budget, so I left it up to the girls whether they wanted to use the makeup artist or not. Most just did their makeup themselves, with coordinating shades and similar styles, and everyone looked beautiful."
~ Shawna J., Portland, OR

## MANICURE/PEDICURE

As a final touch, it's nice to have a professional manicure and/or pedicure the day of or day before your wedding.

**Things to Consider:** Don't forget to bring the appropriate color nail polish with you for your appointment and keep a bottle in case of any chips. You can either go to the salon or have the manicurist meet you at your home or dressing site.

**Price Range:** $15 - $75

### Ideas to Save Money

▶ Try to negotiate getting a manicure or pedicure free of charge or at a discount in exchange for bringing your mother, your fiancé's mother, and your wedding party to the nail salon. Use the time at the salon to laugh and bond before the ceremony.

▶ Consider having a manicure/pedicure party with your wedding party. Provide a few coordinating colors and do each other's nails without the additional cost of going to the salon.

## GROOM'S FORMAL WEAR

The groom should select his formal wear and his attendants' attire based on the formality of the wedding and time of day. The most popular colors are black, white, and gray. Consider darker colors for a fall or winter wedding and lighter colors for a spring or summer wedding.

**Options:** Use the following guidelines to select customary attire for the groom:

Informal wedding:
Business suit
White dress shirt and tie

Semiformal daytime:
Formal suit
White dress shirt
Cummerbund or vest
Four-in-hand or bow tie

**Semiformal evening:**
Formal suit or dinner jacket
Matching trousers
White shirt
Cummerbund or vest
Black bow tie
Cufflinks and studs

**Very formal daytime:**
Cutaway coat
Wing-collared shirt
Ascot
Striped trousers
Cufflinks
Gloves

**Very formal evening:**
Black tailcoat
Matching striped trousers
Bow tie
White wing-collared shirt
Waistcoat
Patent leather shoes
Studs and cufflinks
Gloves

**Things to Consider:** In selecting your formal wear, keep in mind the formality of your wedding, the time of day, and the bride's gown. When selecting a place to rent your tuxedo, check the reputation of the shop. Make sure they have a wide variety of styles to choose from.

Reserve tuxedos for yourself and your ushers several weeks before the wedding to ensure a wide selection and to allow enough time for alterations. Plan to pick up the tuxedos a few days before the wedding to allow time for last-minute alterations in case they don't fit properly. Out-of-town men in your wedding party can be sized at any tuxedo shop. They can send their measurements to you or directly to the shop where you are going to rent your tuxedos.

Ask about the store's return policy and be sure you delegate to the appropriate person (usually your best man) the responsibility of returning all tuxedos within the time allotted. Ushers customarily pay for their own tuxedos.

**Price Range:** $0 - $500

## Ideas to Save Money

▶ Typically, when your wedding party rents their suits or tuxedos from a particular shop, the groom's suit or tux will be free.

▶ For a less formal wedding, the groom may wear a suit he already owns.

▶ Shop at discount retailers, such as Nordstrom Rack, Bluefly.com, eBay, or Overstock.com for a deeply discounted suit. Men's Warehouse sometimes runs a 2-for-1 sale on suits the groom might take advantage of.

▶ Shop for a suit at the end of a season to get deep discounts. For instance, for a summer wedding, buy a linen suit in the fall of the previous year.

## Real Couples' Weddings

▶ "I went to the garment district in Downtown Los Angeles (go on a weekday; Saturday is extremely crowded) and bought an Italian light-wool suit for only $199. I have worn it at least half a dozen times since my wedding, so it was a great investment. By contrast, the Calvin Klein suits I looked at in a tux shop were $160 — to rent."
~ Aaron F., Los Feliz, CA

| APPOINTMENT | Date | Time | Location | Notes |
|---|---|---|---|---|
| Hair Trial Run | | | | |
| Makeup Trial Run | | | | |
| Wedding Day Hair | | | | |
| Wedding Day Makeup | | | | |
| Bridesmaids' Hair | | | | |
| Bridesmaids' Makeup | | | | |
| Nail Salon | | | | |
| Other: | | | | |
| Other: | | | | |
| Other: | | | | |
| Other: | | | | |
| Other: | | | | |
| Other: | | | | |
| Other: | | | | |
| Other: | | | | |
| Other: | | | | |
| Other: | | | | |

## BRIDAL BOUTIQUE COMPARISON CHART

| Questions | POSSIBILITY 1 |
|---|---|
| What is the name of the bridal boutique? | |
| What is the website and e-mail of the bridal boutique? | |
| What is the address of the bridal boutique? | |
| What is the name and phone number of my contact person? | |
| What are your hours of operation? Are appointments needed? | |
| Do you offer any discounts or giveaways? | |
| What major bridal gown lines do you carry? | |
| Do you carry outfits for the mother of the bride? | |
| Do you carry bridesmaids gowns and/or tuxedos? | |
| Do you carry outfits for the flower girl and ring bearer? | |
| What is the cost of the desired bridal gown? | |
| What is the cost of the desired headpiece? | |
| Do you offer in-house alterations? If so, what are your fees? | |
| Do you carry bridal shoes? What is their price range? | |
| Do you dye shoes to match outfits? | |
| Do you rent bridal slips? If so, what is the rental fee? | |
| What is the estimated date of delivery for my gown? | |
| What is your payment policy/ cancellation policy? | |

| POSSIBILITY 2 | POSSIBILITY 3 |
| --- | --- |
|  |  |
|  |  |
|  |  |
|  |  |
|  |  |
|  |  |
|  |  |
|  |  |
|  |  |
|  |  |
|  |  |
|  |  |
|  |  |
|  |  |
|  |  |
|  |  |
|  |  |

## BRIDAL ATTIRE

Bridal Boutique/Store:

Date Ordered:

Salesperson:                              Phone:

Address:

City:                         State:              Zip:

Website:

E-mail:

Description of Dress:

|  | Manufacturer | Style | Size | Cost |
|---|---|---|---|---|
| Wedding Gown |  |  |  |  |
| Headpiece |  |  |  |  |
| Veil/Hat |  |  |  |  |
| Shoes |  |  |  |  |

## GOWN ALTERATIONS

Location:

Cost:

Tailor:                                   Phone:

Address:

City:                   State:              Zip:

Website:

E-mail:

|  | Alteration | Date/Time |
|---|---|---|
| First Alteration |  |  |
| Second Alteration |  |  |
| Third Alteration |  |  |
| Final Alteration |  |  |

Bridal Boutique/Store: _____

Date Ordered: _____

Salesperson: _____ Phone: _____

Address: _____

City: _____ State: _____ Zip: _____

Website: _____

E-mail: _____

Description of Dresses: _____

Cost: _____

Manufacturer: _____

Date Ready: _____

## BRIDESMAIDS' SIZES

| Name | Dress | Height | Bust | Waist | Shoes |
|------|-------|--------|------|-------|-------|
|  |  |  |  |  |  |
|  |  |  |  |  |  |
|  |  |  |  |  |  |
|  |  |  |  |  |  |
|  |  |  |  |  |  |
|  |  |  |  |  |  |
|  |  |  |  |  |  |
|  |  |  |  |  |  |
|  |  |  |  |  |  |
|  |  |  |  |  |  |

## GROOM/GROOMSMEN'S ATTIRE

Store Name:

Date Ordered:

Salesperson:                                    Phone:

Address:

City:                          State:                    Zip:

Website:

E-mail:

Description of Tuxedo/Suit:

Cost:

Manufacturer:

Date Ready:


## GROOM/GROOMSMEN'S SIZES

| Name | Height | Waist | Sleeve | Inseam | Jacket | Neck | Shoes |
|------|--------|-------|--------|--------|--------|------|-------|
|      |        |       |        |        |        |      |       |
|      |        |       |        |        |        |      |       |
|      |        |       |        |        |        |      |       |
|      |        |       |        |        |        |      |       |
|      |        |       |        |        |        |      |       |
|      |        |       |        |        |        |      |       |
|      |        |       |        |        |        |      |       |
|      |        |       |        |        |        |      |       |
|      |        |       |        |        |        |      |       |

# Angela & Nathan

Total Spent: $7,320
April 3, 2009 • Tampa, Florida • 220 guests
Photography by Beulah Polito, http://beulahanne.com

## Budget Breakdown

| | | | |
|---|---|---|---|
| Attire | $750 | Bar | $500 |
| Stationery | $120 | Music | $0 |
| Ceremony & Reception Site | $0 | Bakery | $300 |
| | | Flowers | $700 |
| Photography | $500 | Décor & Rental Items | $500 |
| Videography | $2,000 | Miscellaneous | $150 |
| Food | $1,800 | Total | $7,320 |

Angela and Nathan radiate style and creativity — he's the drummer for the band Anberlin, and they are both part of a small art company called Verdure Studio. They tied the knot in Nathan's parent's beautiful backyard in Tampa, Florida. Angela and Nathan both come from big families, (they're each 1 of 7 kids!), and they wanted to include everyone in the wedding as much as possible. Originally, they didn't have a set budget; they just knew they didn't want to spend a lot of money. Luckily, their big families came in very handy! Help from family and friends kept them from spending more than they wanted to. From the music to the food to the decorations and more, Angela and Nathan's laid-back backyard wedding was all about love, family and tons of personality.

### FROM THE BRIDE
Nathan and his 6 siblings have grown up in the same house in Tampa their entire lives and always said whoever was to get married first "got" the back-yard. Nathan was the one who proposed before anyone else so we were able to claim it! At first we weren't sure if the backyard would work for both the ceremony and reception — but with lots (and lots) of help from both of our families and long-time family friends, we managed to pull it off.

### DECORATIONS & FLOWERS
Friends and family helped decorate the backyard with Chinese lanterns, lights, candles, flowers and more. My main color was yellow with some white and green accents, and the backyard was full of greenery and white and yellow flowers. We purchased mason jars from Publix to hold some of the flowers and white candles. We purchased four sizes of bottles and jars from SpecialtyBottle.com to hold flowers for the centerpieces. Our florist,

Amy Fretto from Grassroots Flowers, did an amazing job, from the centerpieces to the bouquets to the boutonnieres. Really, the backyard is so beautiful that it wasn't hard to make it look good for the wedding.

## ATTIRE

My dress was from Jessica McClintock, and I fell in love with it immediately because it was so different. I loved the tiers and the shape of it — it felt very vintage, which went nicely with my ring! My hairpiece was from Etsy, made by Portobellow. My shoes were from DSW and were supposed to be used for my older sister's wedding but they ended up not matching her dress, so when my wedding rolled around I tried them with my dress and they fit perfectly!

## FOOD

We had a long-time family friend cater, with the help of her husband and sons. This was also a money saver. What we had was basically a "create your own salad" bar with big bowls of lettuce and all different toppings you could add, such as strawberries, peppers and grilled chicken. The sides were baked potatoes — sweet and regular — and wheat rolls or biscuits with homemade apple butter. By having a big salad as your meal, you can save a great deal of money, because it feeds lots of people!

## RENTALS

Our wedding was super laid-back and chill. Everyone, except the bridal party and family, sat wherever. I always thought it was more comfortable at weddings when people didn't have assigned seating, that way you can sit with who you want to and people don't feel confined to one table. Also, it's one less thing to stress over (making a seating chart)! We rented chairs and borrowed a few tables and table cloths from our parents' churches. We also had a firepit set up with chairs around it for people to sit and drink their coffee and talk.

## MUSIC

We did not rent a dance floor. The only real dancing that happened at our wedding was the first dance, and the father-daughter and mother-son dances, which we used the patio for. For music, we made a long playlist of some of our favorite songs and just let it play during the reception.

## VIDEOGRAPHY

The places where we did splurge were things that we felt like we wouldn't

be able to live without. Our friend Daniel Davison used to shoot weddings in Super 8 film for a living. He makes these amazing 20-minute videos of your wedding day that play to music that you choose. My sister had it done for her wedding, and when Nathan and I watched it, we knew we had to have it for our wedding. The only thing is, because Super 8 film is so old, it's really expensive to process. So hiring him was pretty pricey, but *so* worth it. I've watched our wedding DVD about 25 times over now!

There's something amazing about video and being able to go back and relive your wedding day, especially because the day can be somewhat of a blur with so much happening.

## BAR

Another thing that was a splurge and that I would say was pretty unique was the coffee bar we had. We hired this company called Café Ala Carte, and they bring in their own little coffee bar and make fancy coffee drinks for all the guests! It was a huge hit — everyone loved it. Everyone who knows Nathan and me knows that we're huge fans of coffee, so having that at our wedding really gave it a personal touch. As for alcohol, we don't drink a ton, so it made sense for us not to have alcoholic beverages. It was just another expense that would have been unnecessary. And because we had the coffee bar, I don't think anyone noticed or cared that there weren't alcoholic beverages.

## ADVICE

I think what was fun and unique about our wedding is that it was 100 percent our style. People came to our wedding and told us that it was "so us." And I loved that. I feel like a lot of couples get wrapped up in doing the whole "classic wedding" and are afraid of stepping out of the box and doing something different, even if their style isn't necessarily "classic."

My top piece of advice for people with small budgets would be, use the help of your friends and family as much as possible, no matter what the task. Most people think they need to hire someone for every little detail of their wedding, but if you can get away with having friends and family help with things like food and décor, it saves a great deal of money. And be resourceful — see if there are things you already own that you'd like to use as part of the decorations.

# Photography

THE PHOTOGRAPHS TAKEN AT YOUR wedding are the best way to preserve your special day. Chances are you and your fiancé will look at the photos many times during your lifetime. Therefore, hiring a good photographer is one of the most important tasks in planning your wedding.

## BRIDE & GROOM'S ALBUM

The bride and groom's photo album contain the most photographs and will be looked at repeatedly over the years. Choosing a photographer who will shoot your wedding in the style you want and deliver the shots you want is an important task. Photography packages come in a very wide range of prices and services.

Options: Photographers will tell you that they're skilled in "photo journalistic," "candid" or "editorial" style photography, so look through their portfolios for the style that stands out to you. Some photographers are known for formal poses, while others specialize in more candid, creative shots. Some can capture both.

The industry standard for wedding photographers is now digital film, which is the easiest to print, retouch, and allows the photographer to get the most shots to choose from. However, some photographers still like to use film, or a combination of digital and film. Film forces the photographer to choose and set up each shot carefully and artfully and produces a timeless, romantic and textured photograph. Decide which look and feel you want for your photos.

You also want to inquire as to whether your desired photographer works alone or with a backup shooter or assistant. Having more than one person shooting the wedding means you will have a wider variety of shots, especially candids and special moments that one person could miss. Many times a second photographer will be included in the price of the package.

Finally, there are a large variety of wedding albums. They vary in size, color, material, construction and price. Traditional-style albums frame each individual photo in a mat on the page. Digitally designed "Montage" albums group the photos in a creatively designed fashion for a more modern look. Find one that you like and will feel proud of showing to your friends and family. Some of the most popular manufacturers of wedding albums are Art Leather, Leather Craftsman, Capri and Renaissance. Different papers are also available to print your photos — pearl and metallic as well as black and white can be chosen. Ask to see samples.

Compare at least three photographers for quality, value, and price. Be aware that novice photographers or those who shoot weddings "on the side" are less expensive, but the quality of their photographs may not be as good as a wedding professional. For many couples on budgets, the photography was the area in which they splurged in order to have the best wedding album possible.

**Things to Consider:** It is always best to hire a photographer who specializes in weddings. Your photographer should be experienced in wedding procedures and familiar with your ceremony and reception sites. This will allow him or her to anticipate your next move and be in the proper place at the right time to capture all the special moments. However, personal rapport is extremely important. The photographer may be an expert, but if you don't feel comfortable or at ease with him or her, your photography will reflect this. Comfort and compatibility with your photographer can make or break your wedding day and your photographs!

Look at his or her work. See if the photographer captured the excitement and emotion of the bridal couple. Also, remember that the wedding album should unfold like a story book of the wedding day. Discuss with your photographer the photos you want and create a shotlist to ensure that your photographer captures the "must-haves." A good wedding photographer will plan the day with you to ensure that all the important moments are covered.

Consider having a "First Look" session, which is when the bride and groom opt to see each other right before the ceremony. The photographer captures this special, intimate moment, making for beautiful photos. Many couples love First Looks because it puts them at ease before walking down the aisle, as well allows them to skip lengthy portrait sessions between the ceremony and reception. They get to have a private moment together and spend more time with their guests after the ceremony.

When comparing photographer prices, compare the quantity and size of the photographs in your album and the type of album that each photographer will use. Ask how many photos will be taken on average at a wedding of your size. Some photographers do not work with proofs. Rather, they simply supply you with a finished album after the wedding. Doing this may reduce the cost of your album but will also reduce your selection of photographs. Many photographers will put your proofs on a DVD for viewing. This is much less bulky and an easy way to preview all of your wedding photos.

Make sure the photographer you interview is the specific person who will photograph your wedding. Many companies have more than one photographer. The more professional companies will make sure that you meet with (and view the work of) the photographer who will photograph your wedding. This way you can get an idea of his or her style and personality and begin to establish a rapport with your photographer. Your chosen photographer's name should go on your contract!

Be sure to compare the number of hours each photographer includes in their package. Most photographers will begin shooting before the ceremony begins and continuing through the reception, meaning that you will probably need a package that is about 6 to 8 hours for a formal wedding. Photographers charge a lot for extra hours, so be sure you get the coverage you need without feeling rushed or accruing extra charges.

Finally, some churches do not allow photographs to be shot during the ceremony, or they have special guidelines, such as shooting from a specific balcony or from behind the last row of guests. Please find out the rules and present them to your photographer so he or she is knowledgeable about your site. It can be tricky to get beautiful shots and angles if your venue has restrictions, so you should also take that into consideration.

Price Range:  $900 - $9,000

▶ Consider hiring a professional photographer for the formal shots of your ceremony only. You can then ask your guests to take candid shots at the reception and create an online photo album where they can post their favorite shots.

▶ Select a photographer who charges a flat fee to shoot the wedding and includes a DVD of the hi-res photos in his or her package. Many photographers will add this in if you ask.

▶ Hire a photographer who will work for a small fee plus trade, such as building that person a new website in exchange for shooting your wedding.

▶ Consider a photography or art school student who is looking to build or beef up a wedding portfolio. Be sure to view plenty of that person's work to be sure he or she is skilled in framing a shot, finding creative angles, or working in bright or dim lighting.

▶ Lower the cost of your photography package by putting them into an album yourself.

▶ Ask for specials and package deals. Your photographer may be willing to negotiate to get your business, but you won't know if you don't ask.

▶ If you're getting married on a Friday, Sunday or Saturday during the day, you may be able to get a discounted rate from some photographers. Saturday evenings are, of course, the most popular day and time to get married, so any off-peak days or times can mean a savings of up to 20 percent.

▶ Like any contract, always read the fine print on your photographer's contract. You'll want to be fully aware of any extra charges for things like travel, extra hours, special types of album, etc.

▶ "One high-end photographer we met with showed us recent weddings he'd shot, and I didn't see many of the creative and fun candid shots we wanted. He had mostly detail shots and posed portrait photos. When we mentioned it, he said, 'Oh, sure, I can do that — whatever you want.' People will *tell* you they can do anything in hopes of getting your business, but if you don't see it in their portfolio, it's probably not their forté. We went with someone else who was more our style."
~ Leila S., Park City, UT

▶ "Instead of a $3,000 photographer, we hired a less expensive photographer and rented a photobooth for about $1,000. Everyone got one strip of photos for them and one strip for us, which they stuck into an album we set out. Guests loved it, and we were literally crying and laughing as we looked through the album of funny, silly photos later. It was our best idea!"
~ Nina J., Nashville, TN

▶ "Using a photographer who doesn't typically shoot weddings can be a big money saver, just be sure you give him or her a complete list of your must-have shots. You think a picture of the bride with her mother would be an obvious one, but with so much going on, a less-experienced photographer might not remember to get it. That was the case with our wedding photos, and I wished I'd taken the time to make a complete shotlist."
~ Christie S., New Haven, CT

## ENGAGEMENT PHOTOS

Many couples are interested in a set of engagement photos to accompany their wedding-day photography.

Options: Engagement photos make a nice keepsake for the couple, as well as a gift for friends and family. If taken far enough in advance, you can include these photos in your Save the Date cards.

Things to Consider: Modernly, most couples prefer to have engagement photos taken outside and not in a studio. Ask your photographer if he or she can scout locations. Decide whether you want candid shots or posed portrait shots or a combination of both. On the day of the shoot, bring more than one wardrobe change and wear nice shoes, as many shots will be full-body. Engagement shoots usually include affectionate shots such as the couple hugging or even kissing, so talk to your partner about what you're both comfortable with. Finally, ask your photographer to take some classic bridal portraits (shots of just bride).

Price Range: $200 - $750

## Ideas to Save Money

▶ Consider hiring the same photographer for engagement photos as for the wedding; many will build the price into the total photography package.

▶ Ask a friend or family member take photos of you and your fiancé as your engagement photographs.

## Real Couples' Weddings

▶ "A friend who is a budding photographer offered to shoot our wedding free of charge, but we were hesitant to go with an amateur for the actual wedding. Instead, we used him for our engagement photos, which were really fun and looked cute on our Save the Date magnets. One thing to cross off our budget checklist!"
~ Allison B., Reno, NV

## FORMAL BRIDAL PORTRAIT

You may want a studio bridal portrait taken a few weeks before the wedding. Traditionally, this photo was sent to the newspaper to announce a marriage.

Things to Consider: Some fine bridal salons provide an attractive background where the bride may arrange to have her formal bridal photograph taken after the final fitting of her gown. This will save you the hassle of bringing your gown and headpiece to the photographer's studio and dressing up once again.

Price Range: $75 - $300

▶ Consider having your formal portrait taken the day of your wedding. This will save you the studio costs and the hassle of getting dressed for the photo. The photograph will be more natural since the bridal bouquet will be the one you carry down the aisle. Also, brides are always most beautiful on their wedding day!

▶ Feel free to skip the formal bridal portrait if it's not in your budget. Few newspapers still accept these announcements.

## PARENTS' ALBUM

The parents' album is a smaller version of the bride and groom's album. It usually contains about twenty 5x7" photographs. Photos should be carefully selected for each individual family. If given as a gift, the album can be personalized with the bride and groom's names and date of their wedding on the front cover. Small coffeetable-style books can also be created from digital files that are montaged onto the pages. Ask to see samples of different types of parent albums available.

Price Range:  $100 - $600

**Ideas to Save Money**

▶ Try to negotiate at least one free parents' album with the purchase of the bride and groom's album.

**Real Couples' Weddings**

▶ "To save money, we decided to make our parents their own special coffeetable albums using Blurb.com. For about $40 each, we created two really nice-looking hardcover books."
~ Nicole & Steven J., Chicago, IL

## PROOFS/PREVIEWS

Proofs/previews or proof DVDs are the preliminary prints or digital images from which the bride and groom select photographs for their album and for their parents' albums. The prints vary from 4x5" to 5x5" and 4x6". The DVD allows you to view your photos on a screen in a larger size and more detail.

**Things to Consider:** When selecting a package, ask how many photos the photographer will take. The more images, the wider the selection you will have to choose from. For a wide selection, the photographer must take at least 5 times the number of prints that will go into your album.

Ask the photographer how soon after the wedding you will get to see your proofs. Request this in writing. Ideally, the proofs will be ready by the time you get back from your honeymoon. Some photographers may take up to 8 weeks, depending on the season.

Price Range: $100 - $600

### Ideas to Save Money

▶ Don't purchase a proof book in addition to your wedding album to save money.

## DIGITAL FILES & EXTRA PRINTS

Most digital files are "jpegs," which is the file type that most labs use to make prints.

Extra prints are photographs ordered in addition to the main album or parents' albums. These are usually purchased as gifts for the bridal party, close friends and family members. Most photographers will not sell you the digital files up front since they hope to make a profit on selling extra prints after the wedding.

**Things to Consider:** It is important to discuss the cost of extra prints with your photographer since prices vary considerably. Knowing what extra prints will cost ahead of time will help you know if the photographer is truly within your budget. Ask the photographers you interview how long they keep the files and at what point they will become available to you. A professional photographer should keep a backup copy of the digital files for at least 10 years. Once you own your digital files, make a backup copy of your disk every 5 or 6 years, as CDs and DVDs can deteriorate after 8 years or so.

Price Range: $100 - $800

## Ideas to Save Money

▶ Many photographers will sell you the entire set of digital files after all photos have been ordered by family and friends. Often the price will vary, depending on the amount spent on re-orders. You can then make as many prints as you wish for a fraction of the cost.

▶ Find a photographer whose package includes a DVD of all your digital negatives, so you can make as many prints as you like. The only draw-back is that printing photos at high quality and assembling albums is time-consuming, and not every couple will want to do it.

## PHOTOGRAPHER'S INFORMATION SHEET

*Once it is completed, make a copy of this form to give to your photographer as a reminder of your various events.*

**THE WEDDING OF:** _____ **Phone:** _____

### PHOTOGRAPHER'S COMPANY

Business Name: _____

Address: _____

City: _____ State: _____ Zip: _____

Website: _____ E-mail: _____

Photographer's Name: _____ Phone: _____

Assistant's Name: _____ Phone: _____

### ENGAGEMENT PHOTOGRAPH

Date: _____ Time: _____

Location: _____

Address: _____

City: _____ State: _____ Zip: _____

### BRIDAL PORTRAIT

Date: _____ Time: _____

Location: _____

Address: _____

City: _____ State: _____ Zip: _____

*Once it is completed, make a copy of this form to give to your photographer as a reminder of your various events.*

## OTHER EVENTS

Event:

Date:                              Time:

Location:

Address:

City:                              State:        Zip:

## CEREMONY

Date:               Arrival Time:            Departure:

Location:

Address:

City:                              State:        Zip:

Ceremony Restrictions/Guidelines:


## RECEPTION

Date:               Arrival Time:                Departure:

Time:

Location:

Address:

City:                              State:        Zip:

Reception Restrictions/Guidelines:

# PHOTOGRAPHER COMPARISON CHART

| Questions | POSSIBILITY 1 |
|---|---|
| What is the name and phone number of the photographer? | |
| What is the website and e-mail of the photographer? | |
| What is the address of the photographer? | |
| How many years of experience do you have as a photographer? | |
| What percentage of your business is dedicated to weddings? | |
| Approximately how many weddings have you photographed? | |
| Are you the person who will photograph my wedding? | |
| Will you bring an assistant with you to my wedding? | |
| How do you typically dress for weddings? | |
| Do you have a professional studio? | |
| What type of equipment do you use? | |
| Do you bring backup equipment with you to weddings? | |
| Do you need to visit the ceremony and reception sites prior to the wedding? | |
| Do you have liability insurance? | |
| Are you skilled in diffused lighting and soft focus? | |
| Can you take studio portraits? | |
| Can you retouch my images? | |

| POSSIBILITY 2 | POSSIBILITY 3 |
|---|---|
|  |  |
|  |  |
|  |  |
|  |  |
|  |  |
|  |  |
|  |  |
|  |  |
|  |  |
|  |  |
|  |  |
|  |  |
|  |  |
|  |  |
|  |  |
|  |  |
|  |  |

# PHOTOGRAPHER COMPARISON CHART (CONT.)

| Questions | POSSIBILITY 1 |
|---|---|
| Can digital files be purchased? If so, what is the cost? | |
| What is the cost of the package I am interested in? | |
| What is your payment policy? | |
| What is your cancellation policy? | |
| Do you offer a money-back guarantee? | |
| Do you use paper proofs or DVD proofing? | |
| How many photographs will I have to choose from? | |
| When will I get my proofs? | |
| When will I get my album? | |
| What is the cost of an engagement portrait? | |
| What is the cost of a formal bridal portrait? | |
| What is the cost of a parent album? | |
| What is the cost of a 5 x 7 reprint? | |
| What is the cost of an 8 x 10 reprint? | |
| What is the cost of an 11 x 14 reprint? | |
| What is the cost per additional hour of shooting at the wedding? | |

| POSSIBILITY 2 | POSSIBILITY 3 |
|---|---|
| | |
| | |
| | |
| | |
| | |
| | |
| | |
| | |
| | |
| | |
| | |
| | |
| | |
| | |
| | |

## WEDDING PHOTOGRAPHS

*Check off all photographs you would like taken throughout your wedding day. Then make a copy of this form and give it to your photographer.*

### PRE-CEREMONY PHOTOGRAPHS

- ❑ Bride leaving her house
- ❑ Wedding rings with the invitation
- ❑ Bride getting dressed for the ceremony
- ❑ Bride looking at her bridal bouquet
- ❑ Maid of honor putting garter on bride's leg
- ❑ Bride by herself
- ❑ Bride with her mother
- ❑ Bride with her father
- ❑ Bride with mother and father
- ❑ Bride with her entire family and/or any combination thereof
- ❑ Bride with her maid of honor
- ❑ Bride with her bridesmaids
- ❑ Bride with the flower girl and/or ring bearer
- ❑ Bride's mother putting on her corsage
- ❑ Groom leaving his house
- ❑ Groom putting on his boutonniere
- ❑ Groom with his mother
- ❑ Groom with his father
- ❑ Groom with mother and father
- ❑ Groom with his entire family and/or any combination thereof
- ❑ Groom with his best man
- ❑ Groom with his ushers
- ❑ Groom with the bride's father
- ❑ Bride and her father getting out of the limousine
- ❑ Special members of the family being seated
- ❑ Groom waiting for the bride before the processional
- ❑ Bride and her father just before the processional

*Check off all photographs you would like taken throughout your wedding day. Then make a copy of this form and give it to your photographer.*

## OTHER PRE-CEREMONY PHOTOGRAPHS YOU WOULD LIKE

❑ _____

❑ _____

❑ _____

## CEREMONY PHOTOGRAPHS

❑ The processional

❑ Bride and groom saying their vows

❑ Bride and groom exchanging rings

❑ Groom kissing the bride at the altar

❑ The recessional

## OTHER CEREMONY PHOTOS YOU WOULD LIKE

❑ _____

❑ _____

❑ _____

## POST-CEREMONY PHOTOGRAPHS

❑ Bride and groom

❑ Newlyweds with both of their families

❑ Newlyweds with the entire wedding party

❑ Bride and groom signing the marriage certificate

❑ Flowers and other decorations

## OTHER POST-CEREMONY PHOTOS YOU WOULD LIKE

❑ _____

❑ _____

❑ _____

# WEDDING PHOTOGRAPHS

*Check off all photographs you would like taken throughout your wedding day. Then make a copy of this form and give it to your photographer.*

## RECEPTION PHOTOGRAPHS
- ❑ Entrance of newlyweds and wedding party into the reception site
- ❑ Receiving line
- ❑ Guests signing the guest book
- ❑ Toasts
- ❑ First dance
- ❑ Bride and her father dancing
- ❑ Groom and his mother dancing
- ❑ Bride dancing with groom's father
- ❑ Groom dancing with bride's mother
- ❑ Wedding party and guests dancing
- ❑ Cake tables
- ❑ Cake-cutting ceremony
- ❑ Couple feeding each other cake
- ❑ Buffet table and its decoration
- ❑ Bouquet-tossing ceremony
- ❑ Garter-tossing ceremony
- ❑ Musicians
- ❑ The wedding party table
- ❑ The family tables
- ❑ Candid shots of your guests
- ❑ Bride and groom saying goodbye to their parents
- ❑ Bride and groom looking back, waving goodbye in the getaway car

## OTHER RECEPTION PHOTOS YOU WOULD LIKE
- ❑ _____
- ❑ _____
- ❑ _____
- ❑ _____

# Laura & Daniel

Total Spent: $9,925
October 11, 2009 • Torrington, Connecticut • 114 guests
Photography by Ricky Chapman of Public Image Photography,
www.publicimagephotography.com

## Budget Breakdown

| | | | | |
|---|---|---|---|---|
| Attire | $800 | Bar | $500 |
| Stationery | $25 | Music | $0 |
| Ceremony & Reception Site | $0 | Bakery | $400 |
| | | Flowers | $500 |
| Photography | $2,500 | Décor & Rental Items | $2,700 |
| Videography | N/A | Miscellaneous | $200 |
| Food | $2,300 | **Total** | **$9,925** |

On an autumn day in Connecticut, family and friends helped transform the bride's childhood home into the backdrop for a laid-back, romantic wedding full of seasonal touches, flea market treasures and personal mementos. Laura and Daniel's union was a day of easygoing celebration and, although it had been a difficult year in which Laura's father passed away, the couple felt completely surrounded by memories and love. "Having the wedding at my house made me feel closer to my dad. I love that when I look at our wedding photos, even though my dad is not in them, I am surrounded by all things he planted, built, designed and collected." In keeping with that idea, the couple DIYed and thrifted as many aspects as they could to keep costs low. In the end, their event had the feel of an elegant fall picnic, for just under $10,000.

## FROM THE BRIDE

We decided on an October wedding at my family's home in Connecticut. It was important for us to honor my father's memory while still creating a day that was a joyful celebration of our marriage. Ultimately, having the wedding at home created a strong sense of my dad's presence.

We didn't start with a specific budget, but throughout the planning phase tried to keep it as cheap as possible. Our budget limitations forced us to be creative with what we already owned and the natural resources around us. As a result, some of my favorite decorations cost almost nothing. For example, I used my button collection on the placecards and collected sycamore bark from my street for table numbers. Also, I was able to scale back some ideas I had seen on wedding blogs. For instance, I loved the idea of making my own napkins but, because of the cost of fabric and amount of sewing it would require, we chose instead to use squares of fabric to ground our centerpieces. I was happy with the look, and my grandmother (upon Daniel's suggestion) incorporated the fabric into a wedding quilt she made for us.

We knew we wanted an intimate and relaxed wedding so, along with our families, we did most of the work ourselves. Daniel and I scoured antique stores and flea markets for decorations and spent many, many hours working in the yard getting my family's home ready for the wedding. My lovely sisters made and canned apple butter for favors. We also had a large group to help with setup the day before and morning of the wedding. Growing up, my family always hosted large picnics, and I love that our day had the same relaxed and fun feel.

### ATTIRE

We kept attire costs down because the wedding dress I chose was fairly inexpensive, and I didn't wear a veil. Dan wore a black suit, and we ordered personalized ties from Etsy (the ties were screen-printed with lions in honor of our last name, Lyon!). Etsy also allowed us to get nice jewelry and ties for our wedding party without spending too much.

### STATIONERY

For stationery, we found invitations on clearance at TJ Maxx and made the programs ourselves. We used a piece of my father's artwork, a print of birch trees, as the cover of our programs.

## PHOTOGRAPHY

Photography was our splurge. It was important to us to have beautiful images of our big day, and spending more money on our photographer was one of the best decisions we made. We were willing to pay extra for an album, because we doubted that we would take the time to do it ourselves!

## FOOD

Our caterer doesn't specialize in weddings so he was a bit cheaper than normal, plus he was fabulous to work with and was able to help us come up with a menu in our price range. We had a Thanksgiving meal full of seasonal foods.

## BAR

For alcohol, we were able to save money by only serving beer and wine. We had a guest bring Yuengling beer from Pennsylvania (it is not sold in Connecticut), because it is one of our favorite beers, it is cheap and not something we are able to have very often. To add some variety, we also had pumpkin ale and hard cider. For wine, we had a local store send over a selection of moderately priced reds and whites with the agreement that anything unopened could be returned! The owner of the store also gave us a key to his ice chest and tubs to hold the bottles.

## BAKERY

We had pumpkin cake, which was delicious and stayed with the Thanksgiving theme, but only the bottom layer of our cake was real! The top three layers were actually decorated styrofoam. Guests ate a separate sheet cake, but no one knew the difference!

## CEREMONY

For the ceremony, Daniel had the idea to replace lighting a unity candle with planting a tree, to honor my father, who obsessively planted trees, and to symbolize the beginning or our lives together. We chose to plant Mt. Laurel, which was my dad's favorite flower and the inspiration for my name.

## FLOWERS

My very talented sister-in-law did all the floral arrangements. We bought some flowers wholesale online and the rest came from local farms. Choosing to use seasonal flowers was a big part of keeping the budget low. There are a few things to keep in mind when making flowers a DIY project. First, it takes time! Plan to spend most of the day before the wedding, as well as a good chunk of the wedding day arranging and setting up. I wouldn't recommend a bride take this on — leave it to a talented friend or family member! Also, it is important to have a cool place to store the flowers. It was pretty cold the night before our wedding, so we were able to store most of the arrangements in the garage. We did keep the bouquets and boutonnieres in a refrigerator. Overall, we were able to save money by having a family member do the flowers, but it is a project that requires a good amount of planning and knowledge of floral design.

## DECORATIONS

As for decorations, our best resources were thrift stores and antique shops, a few splurges from Etsy, and our backyards. I learned that in New England it is best to visit flea markets at the end of the summer, because the vendors don't want to store their stuff all winter and practically give it away (like two cases of mason jars that we got for $5!). We spent a little more money on the decorations for the head table, including nicer dishes, a personalized birch tube and more expensive flowers. For the guest tables, we used milk bottles, fabric squares and borrowed tea lights. We used the same chairs for the ceremony and reception and guests helped move them to the tent.

## MUSIC

It really helps to have friends and family members who are musicians; they can play and provide sound equipment. We even had a friend run the music during the reception. However, we completely forgot that we would need someone to announce things like the cutting the cake and the First Dance! We enlisted my

sister and brother, although I think they would have been happier with a bit of notice. When not using a DJ or wedding planner it is important to schedule a time for each formal event you want to include and have someone responsible for making announcements, welcoming guests, etc.

## RENTALS

Rentals for the reception were a big expense. To be honest, an at-home wedding is not always the cheapest option. (My sister was married at a historical barn that was cheaper than the cost of all our rentals.) Overall, one of the best ways to save money when planning a wedding is to find a venue that does not include food service. That way there is freedom to be creative with the food or make it a cocktail reception and stay within a budget.

## ADVICE

Overall, because of our time and budget constraints, we had to be flexible when planning. This turned out to be a blessing because some of the things I liked most about our wedding came together when our original idea didn't work out! During the planning stage a friend liked to remind me that it wasn't about the wedding, it was about the marriage. There were times when I had to step back and remember that the important thing was the sacredness of our vows and the joy in our union, not my table decorations. Keeping the celebration of our marriage as the focus allowed me to enjoy the day fully and that joy is what I remember most about our day and what I think shines through in our pictures.

We can't thank our friends and family enough for all of the time, energy and support they gave to us during the planning stage. With their help we were able to create a wedding that was as beautiful as it was joyful.

# Videography

NEXT TO YOUR PHOTO ALBUM,
videography is the best way to
preserve your wedding memories.
Unlike photographs, videography
captures the mood of the wedding
day in motion and sound.

Getting a wedding on video used to mean bright lights, cables, microphones and huge obtrusive cameras. But technology has evolved, and today's videographers have advanced equipment that allows them to film ceremonies with minimal disruption.

Today's wedding videos can also be edited and professionally produced, with music, slow motion, black and white scenes, and many other special features. You have the option of selecting one, two, or three cameras to record your wedding. The more cameras used, the more action your videographer can capture — and the more expensive

the service. An experienced videographer, however, can do a great job with just one camera.

## MAIN VIDEO

You will need to choose the type of video you want. Do you want the footage edited down to a 30-minute film, or do you want an "as it happened" replay? Remember, an edited video will require more time and will therefore be more expensive than just a documentary of the events.

**Options:** There are two basic types of wedding video production:

documentary and cinematic. The documentary type production records your wedding day as it happened, in real time. Very little editing or embellishment is involved. These types of videos are normally less expensive and can be delivered within days after the wedding.

The cinematic type production is more reminiscent of a movie. Although it can be shot with one camera, most good cinematic wedding videos are shot with two cameras, allowing one videographer to focus on the events as they happen while the other gathers footage that will be added later to enhance the final result. This type of video requires more time due to the extensive editing of the footage, which can take up to 40 hours of studio time.

You may wish to have both of these — one straightforward version and another version with all the details and a nice, theatrical flow.

The latest technology includes the option of producing video in high definition. Having your ceremony shot in HD will ensure that you'll be able to enjoy watching your wedding video in a crisp, clear resolution for years to come.

Things to Consider: Be sure to hire a videographer who specializes in weddings and ask to see samples of his or her work. When considering a particular videographer, look at previous weddings the videographer has done. Notice the color and brightness of the screen, as well as the quality of sound. This will indicate the quality of his or her equipment. Note whether the picture is smooth or jerky. This will indicate the videographer's skill level. Ask about special effects such as titles, dissolve, and multiple screens. Find out what's included in the cost of your package so that there are no surprises at the end!

If you will be getting married in a church, find out the church's policies regarding videography. Some churches might require the videographer to film the ceremony from a specific distance.

If you are getting married outside where there may be a lot of background noise, such as at a beach wedding, you will want to ask your videographer about wireless microphones or using multiple microphones so you won't miss one second of your vows.

Finally, as in photography, there are many companies with more than one videographer. These companies may use the work of their best videographer to sell their packages and then send a less experienced videographer to the wedding. Again, don't get caught in this trap! Be sure to interview the videographer who will shoot your wedding so you can get a good idea of his or her style and personality.

If there are special people, events or toasts that you definitely want captured on film, let your videographer know ahead of time. Just like creating a photography shotlist, this helps your videographer know the order of events and the don't-miss moments.

Price Range: $300 - $4,000

## Ideas to Save Money

▶ Compare videographers' quality, value, and price. There is a wide range, and the most expensive is not necessarily the best. The videographer who uses one camera (instead of multiple cameras) is usually the most cost effective and may be all you need.

▶ Consider hiring a company that offers both videography and photography. You might save money by combining the two services. You will also avoid an awkward struggle between your photographer and videographer as they vie for space as your wedding.

▶ To reduce the amount of time you'll need to use the videographer, consider recording the ceremony only.

▶ If you live in a major city, inquire about videographers in a 100-mile radius. Videographers from less-populated areas will charge almost half as much many times, and many will gladly travel to and from your wedding without extra cost.

▶ Ask a family member or close friend to videotape your wedding. Bonus points if the person works with professional camera equipment for his or her job, such as a cameraman at a news station or production house.

▶ Make recording your wedding fun and save money, too! Purchase a few inexpensive handheld cameras (less than $150), such as the Flip camera, for your wedding party to use throughout the event. The footage will be spontaneous and candid and can be easily edited with free software, including adding music.

## TITLES

Titles and subtitles can be edited into your video before or after the filming. Titles are important since 20 years from now you might not remember the exact time of your wedding or the names of your guests. Some videographers charge more for titling. Make sure you discuss this with your videographer and get in writing exactly what titles will be included.

**Options:** Titles can include the date, time, and location of the wedding, the bride and groom's names, and the names of special members of the family and bridal party. Titles may also include special thanks to those who helped with the wedding. You can then send these people copies of your video, which would be a very appropriate and inexpensive gift!

Price Range: $50 - $300

### Ideas to Save Money

▶ Consider asking for limited titles, such as only the names of the bride and groom and the date and time of the wedding.

## EXTRA HOURS

Find out how much your videographer would charge to stay longer than the contracted time. Do this in case your reception lasts longer than expected. Don't forget to get this fee in writing.

Price Range: $35 - $150 per hour

▶ To avoid paying for hours beyond what's included in your selected package, calculate the maximum number of hours you think you'll need and negotiate that number of hours into your package price.

▶ Instruct the videographer to give you a heads up a few minutes before he or she goes into extra hours. That way, you can decide if you want him or her to continue shooting and avoid any surprise charges.

## Real Couples' Weddings

▶ "We put our deposit for our videographer on our credit card months before our wedding. After the wedding, we were furious to learn that he had charged $200 for an hour of extra time without even mentioning it to us. We should have asked for him to tell us when he was nearing overtime."
~ Farah P., Dallas, TX

## PHOTO MONTAGE

A photo montage is a series of photographs set to music on video. The number of photographs in your photo montage depends on the length of the songs and the amount of time allotted for each photograph. A typical song usually allows for 30 to 40 photos. Photo montages are a great way to display and reproduce your photographs. Copies of this video can be made for considerably less than the cost of reproducing photos.

**Options:** Your photo montage can include photos of you and your fiancé growing up, in addition to shots from your rehearsal, wedding day, honeymoon, or any combination thereof.

**Things to Consider:** Send copies of your photo montage video to close friends and family members as mementos of your wedding.

**Price Range: $60 - $300**

▶ There are many websites that allow you to create your own photo montage either for free or at a very low price. You can then transfer your photo montage to a DVD.

## EXTRA COPIES

A videographer can produce higher quality copies than you can. Ask your videographer what the charge is for extra copies.

Price Range: $15 - $50

▶ You can burn DVDs on your computer; however, before making your own copies of your wedding video, be sure to ask your videographer if that is acceptable. Many contracts prohibit it, and doing so could be copyright infringement. Further, your videographer may have encrypted their DVD to prevent you from being able to make a copy of it.

## SAME-DAY EDIT

Some videographers also offer something called a Same-Day Edit, which is a short, 2- to 6-minute compilation video that the videographer shoots before and during the ceremony, then edits onsite and presents at the reception, recapping the highlights of your day. This is always an unexpected treat for guests that will have everyone laughing and crying.

Things to Consider: You will need to have projection equipment and a screen to show your Same-Day Edit video. Check to see if your videographer can provide this equipment, otherwise it will need to be rented.

Price Range: $200 - $1,000

▶ Find a videographer who will build a Same-Day Edit into his or her package.

## VIDEO GUESTBOOK

An alternative to a traditional guestbook is one in which all your guests say hello and offer their well-wishes on camera. If this is a feature you're interested in, your videographer will probably add an additional fee onto your package price.

Things to Consider: A video guestbook can take up a lot of a videographer's time, so schedule it during the cocktail hour or if you have a second shooter.

Price Range: $100 - $500

▶ If you don't want to spring for a video guestbook feature through your videographer, consider setting up a laptop with a webcam at the entrance to the reception. There is software you can buy that allows your guests to record an unlimited number of videos for you. Flip video cameras will also do the trick. Just make sure you print out instructions for your guests.

# VIDEOGRAPHY COMPARISON CHART

| Questions | POSSIBILITY 1 |
| --- | --- |
| What is the name and phone number of the videographer? | |
| What is the website and e-mail address of the videographer? | |
| What is the address of the videographer? | |
| How many years of experience do you have as a videographer? | |
| Approximately how many weddings have you shot? | |
| Are you the person who will shoot my wedding? | |
| Will you bring an assistant with you to my wedding? | |
| Do you shoot in SD or HD? | |
| Do you have a wireless microphone? | |
| Do you bring backup equipment with you? | |
| Do you visit the ceremony and reception sites before the wedding? | |
| Do you edit the video after the event? | |
| Who keeps the raw footage and for how long? | |
| When will I receive the final product? | |
| What do you charge for a montage? Dissolves? Music? Titles? Graphics? | |
| Will I get a master tape and copies? How many? | |
| How long will the final video be? | |
| Will I be able to make copies of the video? | |
| What is the cost of the desired package? | |
| What is your payment/cancellation policy? | |

| POSSIBILITY 2 | POSSIBILITY 3 |
| --- | --- |
|  |  |
|  |  |
|  |  |
|  |  |
|  |  |
|  |  |
|  |  |
|  |  |
|  |  |
|  |  |
|  |  |
|  |  |
|  |  |
|  |  |
|  |  |
|  |  |
|  |  |
|  |  |
|  |  |

## VIDEOGRAPHY SHOTLIST

*Check off all shots and events you would like captured on your wedding day. Then make a copy of this form and give it to your videographer.*

- ❑ Bride getting ready with bridesmaids
- ❑ Exterior shot of ceremony site
- ❑ Interior shots of altar, flowers, etc.
- ❑ Pinning boutonnieres on groom and groomsmen
- ❑ Groom and ushers hanging out
- ❑ Guests arriving at ceremony
- ❑ Bride and bridesmaids arriving
- ❑ Guests being escorted to their seats
- ❑ Groom at the altar
- ❑ Processional
- ❑ Ceremony
- ❑ Recessional
- ❑ Bride and groom toasting with champagne
- ❑ Wedding party toasting and leaving for reception
- ❑ Reception site
- ❑ Details of reception: centerpieces, placecards, etc.
- ❑ Cocktail hour and guests mingling
- ❑ Bride and groom's grand entrance
- ❑ First dance
- ❑ Family dances
- ❑ Bride's father's toast
- ❑ Maid of honor and best man's toasts
- ❑ Guests dancing
- ❑ Guest interviews (if desired)
- ❑ Bouquet and garter toss
- ❑ Cake cutting
- ❑ Last dance
- ❑ Other: _____
- ❑ Other: _____
- ❑ Other: _____
- ❑ Other: _____

# Sara & Matt

Total Spent: $1,960
July 19, 2008 • Allenspark, Colorado • 80 guests
Photography by family & friends

## Budget Breakdown

| | | | | |
|---|---|---|---|---|
| Attire | $20 | | Bar | $452 |
| Stationery | $26 | | Music | $0 |
| Ceremony & Reception Site | $0 | | Bakery | $178 |
| | | | Flowers | $0 |
| Photography | $25 | | Décor & Rental Items | $130 |
| Videography | N/A | | Miscellaneous | $39 |
| Food | $1,090 | | **Total** | **$1,960** |

Sara and Matt decided right from the beginning that their wedding was going to be everything and everyone they wanted and loved and nothing they didn't. Sara says, "We didn't want to obsess about surface details or let the wedding overshadow our relationship. We wanted our wedding to be sincere, authentic, and memorable — a wedding focused on community and connection. We were convinced that we could make it work in a budget-minded, hand-crafted, eco-friendly way." The couple gave themselves a $2,000 budget and set out to plan a weekend-long wedding celebration in the beautiful mountains of Colorado. In the end, their wedding far exceeded their expectations of fun, family, friends and love.

## FROM THE BRIDE

People pretty much thought we were crazy. A wedding for under $2,000? On a Saturday evening? In July? With just seven months of planning? At times, we thought we were crazy, too. But, with the help of good-natured friends and family, a little luck (the rain stayed away), and a solid plan, we managed to pull off a stress-free wedding that was the truest expression of ourselves. It was full of seriously fun quality time with our friends, family, and — most important — each other.

Instead of starting with the details — dress, flowers, invitations — Matt and I took a different approach. We headed to a Mexican restaurant to brainstorm our goals and vision for our wedding. We decided on 8 goals, which included being surrounded by only our closest friends and family, having a wedding that was good for the environment, spending real time with guests, and making all the decisions ourselves so our wedding represented us (which meant no financial contributions from family).

## VENUE

Matt and I had a very difficult time selecting our wedding venue. The mountains of Colorado are a hugely popular wedding destination (especially in the summer), which drives up costs everywhere. We knew that we wanted to be able to rent out an entire place because we wanted all of our friends and family to stay together. In the end, we chose Sunshine Mountain Lodge. The cost of the venue was covered by the fact that we charged guests to stay there — just $25 to $35 per night. Then we came up with the idea of having the ceremony at a bed and breakfast up the road. We found a lovely lake with picnic tables already there. No need to rent chairs!

Next, we asked our friends and family to serve as the photographers, caterers, hair stylists, DJs, bartenders, officiant, and more. Everyone pitched in. We were going to buy my bouquet from Whole Foods, but we realized we could ask a friend to collect wildflowers from the property. And one of my favorite memories took place in the hours before our ceremony. Matt and I worked elbow-to-elbow with our closest friends, chopping stuff for homemade guacamole, seven-layer dip, fajitas, quesadillas and more.

## ATTIRE

For my dress, I wanted something comfortable. I wanted to be able to dance and walk around and hug without limitation. And there it was. On clearance from Target. A white sundress for a mere $15. I did custom embroidery and made a sash from recycled fabric. The groom wore a suit he already had, and I made his tie from fabric I already had.

## WELCOME PICNIC

To spend quality time with everyone, we opted for a Welcome Picnic instead of a traditional rehearsal dinner. In order for it to fit within our strict budget, we had a make-your-own sandwich bar (including organic meat from Whole Foods!), chips, watermelon, iced tea, lemonade, and homemade chocolate cherry dessert with vanilla ice cream. People helped themselves to food and an assortment of fun activities: football, hot-tub, s'mores around the campfire, board games, a swing dancing lesson, and volleyball.

## CEREMONY

We personalized our wedding day with a tree-planting ceremony and a quilt-wrapping to signify unification, the warmth and support of friends and family that are needed to sustain a healthy relationship, the comfort we bring to each other, and the bond between us that will continue to develop. On our wedding website, we asked guests to send us a small piece of fabric. Then, thanks to the help of an Internet tutorial, Matt and I turned them into a quilt.

## RECEPTION

For the reception, we set up tables in a grove of trees, and our guests feasted on homemade fajitas, tamales, guacamole, salsa, nachos, seven-layer dip, black bean and corn salad, frozen margaritas, and six different types of cakes. We had dancing on the patio, while other guests traded their wedding finery for bathing suits. Some trekked to the campfire to tell ghost stories, while others broke out Scrabble and Uno. Guests helped themselves to wedding favors: handmade cilantro seed packets with directions on the front and our personal guacamole recipe on the back.

In the end, the wedding was better than we expected. It wasn't about the dress, the flowers, or the centerpieces. It was about community, connection, commitment, and old-fashioned fun.

## ADVICE

My advice to other couples on a budget is, start with the big picture, not the details. Sit down with your fiancé and figure out what kind of wedding you want. What do you want to be able to say about it when it's over? Develop a list of your goals and vision and then move on to the smaller details. Always ask yourself, "Does this small detail align with my broader goals?" Make decisions accordingly. And remember that no matter what happens with the details (the weather, the vendors, the food), you will be married in the end!

# Stationery & Guest List

DECIDING WHO TO INVITE TO YOUR special event is an important part of planning the perfect wedding with a budget in mind. Naturally, a smaller wedding will be less expensive and allows you more options within your budget.

## GUEST LIST

Start creating your guest list as soon as possible. You want to have all the most important people in your lives present as you celebrate your union.

Ask your parents and the groom's parents for a list of people they would like to invite. You and your fiancé should make your own lists. Determine if you wish to include children; if so, add their names to your list. All children over the age of 16 should receive their own invitation.

Categorize your initial guest list so it is easy to pare down if need be.

Group your guests into three different categories: those who must be invited, those who should be invited, and those who it would be nice to invite. This will help you decide who you definitely want to invite to your wedding.

**Things to Consider:** Naturally, not everyone you invite to your wedding will be able to attend. For a traditional (non-destination) wedding, if you invite over 200 guests, estimate that about 75 percent of your guest list will come. If you are inviting fewer than 200 guests, 80 to 85 percent will RSVP that they will attend. For a destination wedding, expect that 50 to 70 percent of your guest list will attend, depending on whether the wedding is being held in the Continental U.S. or in a foreign country. However, you should always plan for every person on your list to RSVP "Yes," to be on the safe side.

You may also consider creating a "B list" for your guest list. The B list are people you would like to invite in the event that guests from the original list are unable to attend. Plan to send those B invitations out several weeks before the wedding to give those guests time to RSVP.

When making your final guest list, check to be sure that everyone's addresses are current and their names are spelled correctly.

## Ideas to Save Money

▶ You may find that you are over-budget and need to trim the guest list. This is a difficult task — perhaps the most difficult one you'll face during wedding planning. Start by eliminating people who have been included on your guest list out of courtesy — this means people who you went to school with or grew up with but don't stay in touch with, friends of your parents you don't know (unless your parents are paying for the wedding), coworkers, and people who invited you to their weddings. You should never feel obligated to invite anyone.

▶ Consider making your reception "adults-only"; the cost per plate for children, who eat much less, can be nearly as much as the cost for adults.

▶ Allowing everyone on your guest list a "plus one" can get very expensive. Only married friends and family, your attendants, and those in a long-term committed relationship should be told to bring a guest. While it is bad manners for guests to ask to bring a date if one was not indicated on their invitation, it may happen. If this situation does arise, politely explain that you are on a strict budget that, unfortunately, does not allow for extra guests beyond your list. Friends and family will understand.

▶ "When we inquired about the price for kids' food, our caterer told us that it would be $18 a child — for hotdogs and macaroni and cheese! We decided to have an adults-only wedding, except for my husband's niece and nephew, who were the ring bearer and flower girl. I think people understand; plus, they get to enjoy a night out without the kids!"
~ Aimee A., Boston, MA

▶ "We had a hard time trimming our guest list, but our venue only held 150 people. So, we thought about whether we were using our wedding as a way to get closer to some people. Also, there were some people who made our list because we'd been to their weddings, even if we hadn't seen them in the two years since. With those two things in mind, we were able to remove at least 10 people and their dates, saving us considerable money. It would be nice to have everyone you'd like to see there, but it's just not possible unless you have an unlimited budget."
~ Tracy C., San Luis Obispo, CA

## INVITATIONS

Order your invitations at least four months before the wedding. Allow an additional month for engraved invitations. Invitations are traditionally issued by the bride's parents; but if the groom's parents are assuming some of the wedding expenses, the invitations should be in their names also. Mail all invitations at the same time, six to eight weeks before the wedding.

Options: There are three main types of invitations: traditional / formal, contemporary, and informal. The traditional / formal wedding invitation is white, soft cream, or ivory with raised black lettering. The printing is done on the top page of a double sheet of thick quality paper; the inside is left blank. The contemporary invitation is typically an individualized presentation that makes a statement about the bride and groom.

Informal invitations are often printed on the front of a single, heavyweight card and may be handwritten or preprinted. There are three types of printing: engraved, thermography / letterpressing, and offset printing. Engraving is the most expensive, traditional, and formal type of printing. It also takes the longest to complete. In engraved printing, stationery is pressed onto a copper plate, which makes the letters rise slightly from the page. Thermography is a process that fuses powder and ink to create a raised letter. This takes less time than engraving and is less expensive because copper plates do not have to be engraved. Letterpressing uses plates with raised surfaces to press letters into the paper. It is becoming a popular technique for modern invitations. Offset printing, or flat printing, is the least expensive, the quickest to produce, and offers a variety of styles and colors. It is also the least formal.

**Things to Consider:** If all your guests are to be invited to both the ceremony and the reception, a combined invitation may be sent without separate enclosure cards. Order one invitation for each married or cohabiting couple you plan to invite. The officiant and his or her spouse, as well as your attendants, should receive an invitation.

Allow a minimum of two weeks to address and mail the invitations, longer if using a calligrapher or if your guest list is very large. You may also want to consider ordering invitations to the rehearsal dinner, as these should be in the same style as the wedding invitation.

Although some budget wedding books will advise you to save paper and money by sending email invitations, this is never recommended. For one, an email can quickly get lost in guests' inboxes, leaving you to track down dozens of people who don't RSVP. In addition, some older guests may not be email-savvy and will be confused when they don't receive a paper invitation. Invitations can be inexpensive and beautiful, giving your guests something to proudly display in their homes as a reminder of your Big Day.

**Price Range:** $1.50 to $12 each

## Ideas to Save Money

▶ Designing custom invitations suites can get very pricey. Ask a friend who's a designer to create your look or logo for your invitations. Or have him or her illustrate a photo of you. He or she may be happy to do it free as a wedding gift or in exchange for a small fee. Then have the invitations printed yourself.

▶ If you love the look of engraving, opt for letterpressing, which presses the letters into the paper, providing texture and depth, for about 25% less money.

- ► Beware of expensive printing techniques, paper types and extras. Things like engraving, embossing, textured paper, ribbons, rhinestones, boxed invites, and trifolds add up quickly.

- ► Make your Save the Date a simple postcard or magnet. Magnets are especially cost-effective and practical, because they will end up in plain sight on the refrigerator, instead of hidden in a drawer where guests may forget to RSVP.

- ► Pay attention to shipping costs. An invitation that is over- or undersized, an odd shape, or has features that cause the envelopes to be uneven will cost more to mail. According to the USPS website, any letters with the following characteristics will incur a shipping surcharge:

  - It is a square letter
  - It is too rigid – does not bend easily
  - It has clasps, string, buttons, or similar closure devices
  - It has an address parallel to the shorter dimension of the letter
  - It contains items such as pens that cause the surface to be uneven
  - The length divided by height is less than 1.3 or more than 2.5

- ► Your local post office should also offer a Shape-Based Pricing Template, which provides postage guidelines for different mailing sizes. That square invitation may look nice, but it can surprise you by costing a lot in shipping.

- ► Go with one color on a single-panel invitation. One sheet of heavier cardstock looks nicer than a folded invitation on thin cardstock. And printing in more than one color can mean paying 50 percent more. Give the look of multiple colors by using lighter or darker shades of your main color.

- ► Instead of ordering from a stationery store, find a stationer who works "out of home." Not only will you get personal service, you avoid the overhead costs that get passed down to the customer by way of higher prices. These types of stationers may be more difficult to find, so it's best to ask other brides or check forums for recommendations.

▶ Print at home. Buy your own high-quality printer (about $200) and print invitations at home on cardstock or watercolor paper from any art store. The printer is an investment for after the wedding, as well. Or, take your invitations to an inexpensive printer like Kinko's.

▶ Use Seal and Send invitations. Prices start as low as $1.25 per invitation and include invitation wording, addressed response tent card, and a seal to close the response card.

▶ Order approximately 20 percent more stationery than your actual count. You will mess up a few invitations and envelopes, and the cost to order a small number of invites is much higher than purchasing extras from the beginning.

## Real Couples' Weddings

▶ "I chose a simple, beautiful invitation but paid extra to include a single button and ribbon closure. To my surprise, the post office told me there would be extra charges because the envelope wouldn't lie flat and wasn't 'machinable.' There was an extra charge of 20 cents per envelope, so it cost me an extra $40 to mail our invitations."
~ Caroline D., Raleigh, NC

▶ "I love the look of letterpress, but the price — not so much. It was going to cost $800 for just 100 of the invitations I wanted! I'm the crafty, DIY-bride type so I thought, 'I bet I can figure this out myself.' I took several letterpress classes at the local arts college for $80, and then I bought a small letterpress machine for about $150. I spent about $200 on paper. I saved money, had fun and learned a new skill."
~ April H., Los Angeles, CA

▶ "I thought we were saving money by ordering invitations from a catalog, but when they came, the paper quality was cheap and the pink color we chose was horrible. Then, of course, it was too late to start over. If you're doing a mail order, always request a proof sample or look at invitations at stationery stores in person so you can get a feel for the weight and quality of different paper types."
~ Barbara S., St. Cloud, MN

# RESPONSE CARDS

Response cards are enclosed with the invitation to determine the number of people who will be attending your wedding. They are the smallest card size accepted by the postal service and should be printed in the same style as the invitation. Include a self-addressed and stamped return envelope to make it easy for your guests to return the response cards.

**Things to Consider:** Each couple, each single person, and all children over the age of 16 should receive their own invitation. Indicate on the inner envelope if they may bring an escort or guest. The omitting of children's names from the inner envelope infers that the children are not invited.

### Samples of wording for response cards:

M_____
(The M may be eliminated from the line,
especially if many Drs. are invited)
____ accepts
____ regrets
Saturday the fifth of July
Oceanside Country Club

OR

The favor of your reply is requested
by the twenty-second of May
M_____
will _____ attend

Price Range:   $0.40 - $1 each

## Ideas to Save Money

▶   Instead of paying to have your return address printed on each envelope, buy a stamp with your address. Sites like Etsy.com sell handmade custom stamps in beautiful script-style fonts.

▶   Make your response card a stamped postcard with no envelope to avoid paying for and printing the envelope.

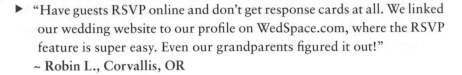

▶ "Have guests RSVP online and don't get response cards at all. We linked our wedding website to our profile on WedSpace.com, where the RSVP feature is super easy. Even our grandparents figured it out!"
~ Robin L., Corvallis, OR

## RECEPTION CARDS

If the guest list for the ceremony is larger than that for the reception, a separate card with the date, time and location for the reception should be enclosed with the ceremony invitation for those guests also invited to the reception. Reception cards should be placed in front of the invitation, facing the back flap and the person inserting them. They should be printed on the same quality paper and in the same style as the invitation itself.

**Sample of an informal reception card:**

Reception immediately following the ceremony
Oceanside Country Club
2020 Waterview Lane
Oceanside, California

**Sample of a formally worded reception card:**

Mr. and Mrs. Alexander Waterman Smith
request the pleasure of your company
Saturday, the third of July
at three o'clock
Oceanside Country Club
2020 Waterview Lane
Oceanside, California

Price Range: $0.40 - $1 each

▶ If the ceremony and reception are in the same location, include the reception information on the invitation and eliminate the reception card. This will save printing and postage costs.

## PEW CARDS

Pew cards may be used to let special guests and family members know they are to be seated in the reserved section on either the bride's side or the groom's side. Guests should take this card to the ceremony and show it to the ushers, who should then escort them to their seats.

Options: Pew cards may indicate a pew number if specific seats are assigned, or may read "Within the Ribbon" if pews are reserved, but no specific seat is assigned.

Things to Consider: These may be inserted along with the invitation, or may be sent separately after the RSVPs have been returned. It is easier to send them after you have received all RSVPs so you know how many reserved pews will be needed.

Price Range: $0.25 - $1 each

▶ Pass on pew cards if you're not having a formal church ceremony and a large wedding.

## SEATING/PLACE CARDS

Seating/place cards are used to let guests know where they should be seated at the reception and are a good way of putting people together so they feel most comfortable. Each card should correspond to a table — either by number, color, or other identifying theme, such as the couples' favorite travel destinations or movie titles. Each table should be marked accordingly.

Things to Consider: Place cards should be laid out alphabetically on a table at the entrance to the reception.

**Price Range:** $0.25 - $1 each

▶ Get creative with seating/place cards; instead of having them printed, write guests' names and tables on a pressed leaf, shell or river rock.

▶ Write guests' names and tables on a board or hand-painted sign. Chalkboard paint, which is less than $15 a can, will turn any flat surface into one to write on.

### Real Couples' Weddings 💬

▶ "I had seen wine cork place card holders for 60 cents each, which seemed pricey, so I DIYed them instead. I bought 200 wine corks in bulk for about $50, then carefully sliced a slit into each one and sanded the bottoms flat so they would sit upright. We printed inexpensive cards with our guests' names and seating arrangements and slid them into the corks. If you have enough time, you could also save your own corks, and ask family and friends to save theirs as well."
~ Karen L., Tampa, FL

## MAPS

Maps to the ceremony and/or reception are frequent inserts in wedding invitations. They need to be drawn and printed in the same style as the invitation and are usually on a small, heavier card.

**Options:** Maps should include both written and visual instructions, keeping in mind the fact that guests may be coming from different locations.

**Price Range:** $0.50 - $1 each

### Ideas to Save Money 💲

▶ There are many websites that allow you to create custom maps for no charge. Print maps on heavier cardstock.

- Ushers can hand out maps to the reception venue at the ceremony to save on the cost of shipping.

- "Including a map to the venue and a list of local activities was going to bump up the cost of mailing our invitations, so we decided to make a wedding website with the same information. Free!"
  ~ Jennifer J., Lake Tahoe, NV

## CEREMONY PROGRAMS

Ceremony programs add a personal touch to your wedding and are a convenient way of letting guests know who your attendants, officiant, and ceremony musicians are, as well as who might be speaking.

Options: Ceremony programs can be handed out by the ushers, or they can be placed at the back of the church for guests to take as they enter.

Price Range: $0.75 - $3 each

**Ideas to Save Money**

- Since programs will generally be looked at and left behind after the ceremony, you can make these yourself to save money on expensive printing. Using a nice script font, print programs on cardstock or watercolor paper. Add a ribbon or other small decoration.

## ANNOUNCEMENTS

Announcements are not obligatory but serve a useful purpose. They may be sent to friends, extended family, or work colleagues who are not invited to the wedding because the number of guests must be limited or because they live too far away. They may also be sent to acquaintances who, while not particularly close to the family, might still want to know about the marriage.

Announcements are also appropriate for friends and acquaintances who are not expected to attend and for whom you do not want to give an obligation of sending a gift. They are in the same look and style of the invitation suite and provide similar information (date, location, etc.), but are sent after the wedding has already taken place.

**Things to Consider:** Announcements should never be sent to anyone who has received an invitation to the ceremony or the reception. They should be addressed before the wedding and mailed the day of or the day after the ceremony.

**Price Range:** $0.75 - $2 each


## THANK-YOU NOTES

Regardless of whether the bride has thanked the donor in person or not, she must write a thank-you note for every gift received.

**Things to Consider:** Order thank-you notes along with your other stationery at least four months before your wedding. You should order some with your maiden initials for thank-you notes sent before the ceremony, and the rest with your married initials for notes sent after the wedding and for future use.

Send thank-you notes within two weeks of receiving a gift that arrives before the wedding, and within two months after the honeymoon for gifts received on or after your wedding day. Be sure to mention the gift you received in the body of the note and let the person know how much you like it and what you plan to do with it.

**Price Range:** $0.40 - $0.75 each


## STAMPS

Don't forget to budget stamps for response cards as well as for invitations!

**Things to Consider:** Don't order stamps until you have had the post office weigh your completed invitation. It may exceed the size and weight for one stamp.

You can also order personalized stamps that fit the occasion. Many websites allow you to place a personal photo on a U.S. stamp of any value, including postage for square envelopes and postcards. Just be aware that customized photo stamps will run about $1 per stamp.

**Price Range:** $0.39 - $1 each

## Ideas to Save Money

▶ Consider the cost of mailing your invitations when you choose their shape and size. For instance, a square invitation will cost more than one stamp to mail, so you may want to opt for a conventional size and shape instead.

## CALLIGRAPHY

Calligraphy is a form of elegant handwriting often used to address invitations for formal occasions. Traditional wedding invitations should be addressed in black or blue fountain pen.

**Options:** You may address the invitations yourself, hire a professional calligrapher, or have your invitations addressed using calligraphy by computer. Make sure you use the same method or person to address both the inner and outer envelopes.

**Price Range:** $0.50 - $3 each

## Ideas to Save Money

▶ You may want to consider taking a short course to learn the art of calligraphy so that you can address your own invitations.

▶ If you have a computer with a laser printer, you can address the invitations yourself using one of many beautiful calligraphy fonts. There are also many free fonts that you can download online for personal use.

► "Who wants to pay $10 an invitation? For $150 total, three of my girlfriends and I took a class from a woman who owns a calligraphy studio and has been hand-lettering for 30 years. Then we had a series of calligraphy 'parties' and hand-lettered all my envelopes. I will say that this isn't a project for a big guest list. One hundred invitations took us three weekends of work!"

~ Meredith R., Tampa, FL

## NAPKINS/MATCHBOOKS

Napkins and matchbooks may also be ordered from your stationer. These are placed around the reception room as decorative items and mementos of the event.

**Things to Consider:** Napkins and matchbooks can be printed in your wedding colors, or simply white with gold or silver lettering. Include both of your names and the wedding date. You may consider including a phrase or thought, or a small graphic design above your names.

**Price Range:** $0.50 - $1.50 each

► Napkins and matchbooks do not have to be customized if budget does not allow for it.

*Make as many copies of this form as needed to accommodate
the size of your guest list.*

**Name:** _____

Arrival Date: _____  Time: _____

Airline: _____  Flight No.: _____

Pick Up By: _____

Will Stay At: _____

Phone: _____

Cost Per Room: _____  Confirmation No.: _____

Departure Date: _____  Time: _____

Taken By: _____

Airline: _____

Flight No.: _____


**Name:** _____

Arrival Date: _____  Time: _____

Airline: _____  Flight No.: _____

Pick Up By: _____

Will Stay At: _____

Phone: _____

Cost Per Room: _____  Confirmation No.: _____

Departure Date: _____  Time: _____

Taken By: _____

Airline: _____

Flight No.: _____

**The Marriage of
Carol Ann Smith and William James Clark
the eleventh of March
San Diego, California**

**OUR CEREMONY**

**Prelude:**
*All I Ask of You,* by Andrew Lloyd Webber

**Processional:**
*Canon in D Major,* by Pachelbel

Rite of Marriage

Welcome guests

Statement of intentions

Marriage vows

Exchange of rings

Blessing of bride and groom

Pronouncement of marriage

Presentation of the bride and groom

**Recessional:**
*Trumpet Voluntary,* by Jeromiah Clarke

## OUR WEDDING PARTY

### Maid of Honor:
Susan Smith, Sister of Bride

### Best Man:
Brandt Clark, Brother of Groom

### Bridesmaids:
Janet Anderson, Friend of Bride
Lisa Bennett, Friend of Bride

### Ushers:
Mark Gleason, Friend of Groom
Tommy Olson, Friend of Groom

### Officiant:
Father Henry Thomas

## OUR RECEPTION

Please join us after the ceremony
in the celebration of our marriage at:
La Valencia Hotel
1132 Prospect Street
La Jolla, California

## STATIONERY COMPARISON CHART

| Questions | POSSIBILITY 1 |
|---|---|
| What is the name and phone number of the stationery provider? | |
| What is the website and e-mail of the stationery provider? | |
| What is the address of the stationery provider? | |
| How many years of experience do you have? | |
| What lines of stationery do you carry? | |
| What types of printing processes do you offer? | |
| How soon in advance does the order have to be placed? | |
| What is the turnaround time? | |
| What is the cost of the desired invitation? Announcement? | |
| What is the cost of the desired response card? Reception card? | |
| What is the cost of the desired thank-you note? | |
| Can I see a proof of my invitation? What is the cost? | |
| What is the cost of the desired wedding program? | |
| What is the cost of addressing the envelopes in calligraphy? | |
| What is your payment policy? | |
| What is your cancellation policy? | |

| POSSIBILITY 2 | POSSIBILITY 3 |
|---|---|
|  |  |
|  |  |
|  |  |
|  |  |
|  |  |
|  |  |
|  |  |
|  |  |
|  |  |
|  |  |
|  |  |
|  |  |
|  |  |
|  |  |
|  |  |

## STATIONERY INFORMATION

**Stationer:** _____ Date Ordered: _____

Salesperson: _____ Phone: _____

Address: _____

City: _____ State: _____ Zip: _____

E-mail: _____


**Stationery Item:**
**(Include selections for Quantity, Cost, Paper, Style, Color, Font)**

Invitations/Envelopes: _____

_____

Response Cards/Envelopes: _____

_____

Reception Cards: _____

Ceremony Cards: _____

Pew Cards: _____

Seating/Place Cards: _____

_____

Rain Cards: _____

Maps: _____

Ceremony Programs: _____

_____

Announcements: _____

Thank-You Notes: _____

Napkins: _____

Matchbooks: _____

Invitations:

Announcements:

Reception Cards:

Response Cards:

Seating/Place Cards

Napkins/Matchbooks:

## GUEST & GIFT LIST

*Make as many copies of this form as needed.*

**Name:** _____

Address: _____

City: _____ State: _____ Zip: _____

Phone: _____

Email: _____

Table/Pew #: _____

Shower Gift: _____ ❏ Thank-You Note Sent

Wedding Gift: _____ ❏ Thank-You Note Sent


**Name:** _____

Address: _____

City: _____ State: _____ Zip: _____

Phone: _____

Email: _____

Table/Pew #: _____

Shower Gift: _____ ❏ Thank-You Note Sent

Wedding Gift: _____ ❏ Thank-You Note Sent


**Name:** _____

Address: _____

City: _____ State: _____ Zip: _____

Phone: _____

Email: _____

Table/Pew #: _____

Shower Gift: _____ ❏ Thank-You Note Sent

Wedding Gift: _____ ❏ Thank-You Note Sent

*Make as many copies of this form as needed.*

**Name:**

Address:

City:                              State:              Zip:

Phone:

Email:

**Name:**

Address:

City:                              State:              Zip:

Phone:

Email:

**Name:**

Address:

City:                              State:              Zip:

Phone:

Email:

**Name:**

Address:

City:                              State:              Zip:

Phone:

Email:

# WEDDING PLANNING NOTES

........................................................................................................

........................................................................................................

........................................................................................................

........................................................................................................

........................................................................................................

........................................................................................................

........................................................................................................

........................................................................................................

........................................................................................................

........................................................................................................

........................................................................................................

........................................................................................................

........................................................................................................

........................................................................................................

........................................................................................................

........................................................................................................

........................................................................................................

........................................................................................................

........................................................................................................

........................................................................................................

........................................................................................................

........................................................................................................

........................................................................................................

# Addressing Invitations

WE RECOMMEND YOU START ADDRESSING your invitations at least three months before your wedding. You may want to ask your maid of honor or bridesmaids to help you with this time-consuming task, as this is traditionally part of their responsibilities.

Organize a luncheon or late afternoon get together with hors d'oeuvres and make a party out of it! If you are working with a wedding consultant, he or she can also help you address invitations.

There are typically two envelopes that need to be addressed for wedding invitations: an inner envelope and an outer envelope. The inner envelope is placed unsealed inside the outer envelope, with the flap away from the person inserting.

The invitation and all enclosures are placed inside the inner envelope facing the back flap. The inner envelope contains the name (or names) of the person (or people) who are invited to the ceremony and/or reception. The address is not included on the inner envelope.

The outer envelope contains the name (or names) and address of the person (or people) to whom the inner envelope belongs.

Use the following guidelines to help you properly address both the inner and outer envelopes.

# GUIDELINES FOR ADDRESSING INVITATIONS

Note: Inner envelope does not include first names or addresses.
The outer envelope includes first names and addresses.

## Husband and Wife (with same surname)
Inner Envelope:   Mr. and Mrs. Smith
Outer Envelope:   Mr. and Mrs. Thomas Smith
                  (use middle name, if known)

## Husband and Wife (with different surnames)
Inner Envelope:   Ms. Banks and Mr. Smith
                  (wife first)
Outer Envelope:   Ms. Anita Banks
                  Mr. Thomas Smith (wife's name & title above
                  husband's)

## Husband and Wife (wife has professional title)
Inner Envelope:   Dr. Smith and Mr. Smith (wife first)
Outer Envelope:   Dr. Anita Smith Mr. Thomas Smith
                  (wife's name & title above husband's)

## Husband and Wife (with children under 16)
Inner Envelope:   Mr. and Mrs. Smith
                  John, Mary, and Glen (in order of age)
Outer Envelope:   Mr. and Mrs. Thomas Smith

## Single Woman (regardless of age)
Inner Envelope:   Miss/Ms. Smith
Outer Envelope:   Miss/Ms. Beverly Smith

## Single Woman and Guest
Inner Envelope:   Miss/Ms. Smith
                  Mr. Jones (or "and Guest")
Outer Envelope:   Miss/Ms. Beverly Smith

## Single Man
Inner Envelope:   Mr. Jones (Master for a young boy)
Outer Envelope:   Mr. William Jones

Note: Inner envelope does not include first names or addresses.
The outer envelope includes first names and addresses.

### Single Man and Guest

Inner Envelope:    Mr. Jones
                   Miss/Ms. Smith (or "and Guest")
Outer Envelope:    Mr. William Jones

### Unmarried Couple Living Together

Inner Envelope:    Mr. Knight and Ms. Orlandi
                   (names listed alphabetically)
Outer Envelope:    Mr. Michael Knight
                   Ms. Paula Orlandi

### Two Sisters (over 16)

Inner Envelope:    The Misses Smith
Outer Envelope:    The Misses Mary and Jane Smith
                   (in order of age)

### Two Brothers (over 16)

Inner Envelope:    The Messrs. Smith
Outer Envelope:    The Messrs. John and Glen Smith
                   (in order of age)

### Brothers & Sisters (over 16)

Inner Envelope:    Mary, Jane, John & Glen
                   (name the girls first, in order of age)
Outer Envelope:    The Misses Smith
                   The Messrs. Smith
                   (name the girls first)

### A Brother and Sister (over 16)

Inner Envelope:    Jane and John
                   (name the girl first)
Outer Envelope:    Miss Jane Smith and
                   Mr. John Smith
                   (name the girl first)

## GUIDELINES FOR ADDRESSING INVITATIONS

Note: Inner envelope does not include first names or addresses. The outer envelope includes first names and addresses.

### Widow
Inner Envelope:   Mrs. Smith
Outer Envelope:   Mrs. William Smith

### Divorcee
Inner Envelope:   Mrs. Smith
Outer Envelope:   Mrs. Jones Smith
                           (maiden name and former husband's surname)


## SAMPLES OF TRADITIONAL/FORMAL INVITATIONS

1) When the bride's parents sponsor the wedding:

> Mr. and Mrs. Alexander Waterman Smith
> request the honor of your presence
> at the marriage of their daughter
> Carol Ann
> to
> Mr. William James Clark
> on Saturday, the fifth of August
> two thousand eight
> at two o'clock in the afternoon
> Saint James by-the-Sea
> La Jolla, California

2) When the groom's parents sponsor the wedding:

> Mr. and Mrs. Michael Burdell Clark
> request the honor of your presence
> at the marriage of
> Miss Carol Ann Smith
> to their son
> Mr. William James Clark

3) When both the bride and groom's parents sponsor the wedding:

Mr. and Mrs. Alexander Waterman Smith
and
Mr. and Mrs. Michael Burdell Clark
request the honor of your presence
at the marriage of their children
Miss Carol Ann Smith
to
Mr. William James Clark

OR

Mr. and Mrs. Alexander Waterman Smith
request the honor of your presence
at the marriage of their daughter
Carol Ann Smith
to
William James Clark
son of Mr. and Mrs. Michael Burdell Clark

4) When the bride and groom sponsor their own wedding:

The honor of your presence is requested
at the marriage of
Miss Carol Ann Smith
and
Mr. William James Clark

OR

Miss Carol Ann Smith
and
Mr. William James Clark
request the honor of your presence
at their marriage

## GUIDELINES FOR ADDRESSING INVITATIONS

5) With divorced or deceased parents:

a) When the bride's mother is sponsoring the wedding and is not remarried:

Mrs. Julie Hurden Smith
requests the honor of your presence
at the marriage of her daughter
Carol Ann

b) When the bride's mother is sponsoring the wedding and has remarried:

Mrs. Julie Hurden Booker
requests the honor of your presence
at the marriage of her daughter
Carol Ann Smith

OR

Mr. and Mrs. John Thomas Booker
request the honor of your presence
at the marriage of Mrs. Booker's daughter
Carol Ann Smith

c) When the bride's father is sponsoring the wedding and has not remarried:

Mr. Alexander Waterman Smith
requests the honor of your presence
at the marriage of his daughter
Carol Ann

d) When the bride's father is sponsoring the wedding and has remarried:

Mr. and Mrs. Alexander Waterman Smith
request the honor of your presence
at the marriage of Mr. Smith's daughter
Carol Ann

6) With deceased parents:

a) When a close friend or relative sponsors the wedding:

>Mr. and Mrs. Brandt Elliott Lawson
>request the honor of your presence
>at the marriage of their granddaughter
>Carol Ann Smith

7) In military ceremonies, the rank determines the placement of names:

a) Any title lower than sergeant should be omitted. Only the branch of service should be included under that person's name:

>Mr. and Mrs. Alexander Waterman Smith
>request the honor of your presence
>at the marriage of their daughter
>Carol Ann
>to
>William James Clark
>United States Army

b) Junior officers' titles are placed below their names and are followed by their branch of service:

>Mr. and Mrs. Alexander Waterman Smith
>request the honor of your presence
>at the marriage of their daughter
>Carol Ann
>to
>William James Clark
>First Lieutenant, United States Army

## GUIDELINES FOR ADDRESSING INVITATIONS

c) If the rank is higher than lieutenant, titles are placed before names, and the branch of service is placed on the following line:

Mr. and Mrs. Alexander Waterman Smith
request the honor of your presence
at the marriage of their daughter
Carol Ann
to
Captain William James Clark
United States Navy

## SAMPLE OF A LESS FORMAL/MORE CONTEMPORARY INVITATION

Mr. and Mrs. Alexander Waterman Smith
would like you to
join with their daughter
Carol Ann
and
William James Clark
in the celebration of their marriage

For additional wording suggestions, log on to www.WedSpace.com

# Melissa & Matthew

Total Spent: $10,000
April 26, 2008 • Brooklyn, New York • 88 guests
Photography by David Abel, www.davidabelphotography.com

## Budget Breakdown

| | | | | |
|---|---|---|---|---|
| Attire | $570 | Bar | $600 |
| Stationery | $500 | Music | $1,000 |
| Ceremony & Reception Site | $4,000 | Bakery | N/A |
| | | Flowers | $80 |
| Photography | $0 | Décor & Rental Items | $0 |
| Videography | N/A | Miscellaneous | $50 |
| Food | $3,200 | **Total** | **$10,000** |

**Melissa and Matthew's wedding day** was a complete reflection of them as a couple — a unique, stylish celebration in the heart of Brooklyn. They took advantage of local resources, such as New York City's famed flower district, and were enterprising when it came to finding nontraditional vendors who would give them great deals and amazing service. They didn't want "cookie-cutter wedding stuff," Matthew explains, so they focused on infusing their personalities into every detail, while sticking to a reasonable budget. In the end, they had a wedding that their friends still talk about.

## FROM THE GROOM

We wanted our wedding day to be about personality, not formality. The sooner the bride and groom acknowledge that getting married is about their love and not the list of wedding "must-haves," the easier it is to enjoy the day and avoid the "I have to have ..." mentality.

## STATIONERY

Our invite was custom-designed and gorgeous. It became the thematic centerpiece for our entire event. We found a local designer to do something unique and totally us. Calligraphy is expensive and, honestly, most people are going to look at your envelope for 2 seconds and throw it away. We paid to have our return address on the back flap, got about 100 times more envelopes than we actually needed (they're cheap), and addressed them with a nice font on our home printer.

## ATTIRE

My actually wife borrowed a friend's $6,000 Monique Lhuillier gown. Find a friend or put an ad on Craigslist to borrow one, and the most you'll have to spend is on the cleaning bill before you return it.

My wife convinced me to buy a nice suit that I could wear for many years. I went to Men's Warehouse and got a "last-year's line" suit that I have worn to six other weddings, two funerals, and one heck of a cocktail party.

## FOOD

We were realistic about our budget and informed the caterers we met right away. We looked locally for someone who didn't do cookie-cutter wedding food. (Most couples will pay silly amounts of money for anything when it's their big day, and wedding caterers are happy to oblige by making a plate of Italian cookies cost $700.) We didn't want a sit-down dinner; weddings are a party, a celebration. We had a cocktail party, but there was plenty of food, and nobody went hungry.

## VENUE

The ceremony and reception were held at the Brooklyn Historical Society, a somewhat nontraditional space that was beautiful. Our guests were amazed, and it reflected our love for Brooklyn and its history.

## BAR

Our caterer was willing to provide bar service (bartender, mixers, ice, glasses) and we provided the booze. Talk to your local liquor store, let them know in advance how much you want to spend, and they'll help you out. Most will also accept buy-backs if you have any unopened bottles after the event.

## MUSIC

We were out for barbecue one night and heard '80s Gone South, a local band that does '80s pop hits in a cool, danceable, country Western style. Turns out we

have some mutual friends, and they decided to do the gig for us for half their usual fee. Find what you like, ask for it, and you'll be surprised how many people are excited to be part of your wedding.

## FLOWERS

We wanted fresh, simple flowers in large arrangements all over the room. We went to the NYC flower district the morning of the wedding and bought heaps of lilac. The cost of all the lilac and vases was cheaper than just *two* arrangements florists quoted us, and smaller clippings and floral tape became boutonnieres. The DIY trimming and arranging was fun for our wedding party.

## PHOTOGRAPHY

Find an aspiring photojournalist. Not only will he or she be thrilled to do it, but you'll get more editorial, candid shots of the wedding. Our photographer, David Abel, needed some NYC shots for his portfolio. We told him the photos that we wanted staged and the rest of the shots were candid, elegant and beautiful. He found the real moments worth capturing between people instead of textbook wedding shots.

## ADVICE

Don't listen to people who tell you that you must do x, y and z. A wedding is a celebration of love, a merging of families, the beginning of a start together, and a wonderful occasion. Remember that there are thousands of gay and lesbian couples in this country who love each other just as much, and they aren't even allowed to do what you're doing. Be thankful, be humble, and be joyful. Whatever you decide to do will be wonderful!

# Reception

THE RECEPTION IS A PARTY WHERE ALL YOUR guests come together to celebrate your new life as a married couple. It should reflect and complement your ceremony. The selection of a reception site will depend on its availability, price, proximity to the ceremony site, and the number of people it will accommodate.

## RECEPTION SITE FEE

There are two basic types of reception sites. The first type charges a per person fee that includes the facility, food, tables, silverware, china, and so forth. Examples: hotels, restaurants, and catered yachts. The second type charges a room rental fee and you are responsible for providing the food, beverages, linens, and possibly tables and chairs. Examples: clubs, halls, parks, museums, and private homes.

The advantage of the first type is that almost everything is done for you. The disadvantage, however, is that your choices of food, china, and linen are limited. Usually you are not permitted to bring in an outside caterer and must select from a predetermined menu. Being allowed to bring in your own caterer and alcohol can save a lot of money.

Options: Private homes, gardens, hotels, clubs, restaurants, halls, parks, museums, yachts, and wineries are some of the more popular choices for receptions.

Things to Consider: When comparing the cost of different locations, consider the rental fee, food, beverages, parking, gratuity, setup charges, and the cost of rental equipment needed, such as tables, chairs, canopies, and so forth. Be sure to get everything included in your price in writing and ask about extra, hidden fees. If your venue is a hotel ballroom, get the exact room in writing. Some hotels will reserve the right to move your wedding to a smaller room to accommodate another party.

If you are planning an outdoor reception, be sure to rent a tent or have a backup site in case of rain. If the price of a tent is out of your budget, see if there is another couple renting your venue that same weekend who is willing to share the cost with you. Many venues will have an indoor reception area in the event of bad weather.

Backyard weddings are very popular for couples with a tight budget because it saves on a rental fee. If a close friend or family member will offer his or her home for your reception, this can be a money-saving option. However, be aware that having a backyard wedding isn't without its costs and caveats. You will need to consider how you will provide or rent tables, chairs, linens, place settings, lighting, a dance floor, parking (if the home doesn't have ample space for parking), restrooms (if the host doesn't want guests inside the home), and space for food prep, cooking and storage. You will also want to be sure the home is covered under the person's homeowner's insurance, in case of an accident. If you do decide to have a backyard wedding however, it can be a memorable and personal reception venue.

Price Range:  $300 - $5,000

## Ideas to Save Money

▶ Since the cost of the reception is approximately 35% of the total cost of your wedding, you can save the most money by limiting your guest list. A sit-down dinner can easily cost $100 a head, so cutting just 10 people from your guest list could save $1,000.

▶ Get married on a Friday, Sunday or in the offseason, which is late-October through February. Venues rent for much less on days other than Saturday evenings. You may be able to save between $300 and $1,000 by not having a Saturday evening wedding. Just be conscious of the fact that guests will need to take extra time off work to attend your wedding and this may affect who can attend. Additionally, some venues limit how late music can be played at a Sunday evening reception.

- Find a venue that lets you bring in your own caterer, which can save a lot of money. A venue with a set list of caterers means limited choices and limited ability to negotiate. For instance, they may not allow you to substitute a dish or take an hors d'oeurve off the menu. However, if you are permitted to hire any caterer you want, you can shop around for the best prices, hire a restaurant that doesn't typically do weddings, choose an hors d'oeurves-only reception, or opt for a less expensive type of food, such as barbecue.

- Consider a brunch wedding with mimosas, a waffle bar and omelet station, or a picnic or garden party wedding, held outdoors and featuring finger sandwiches, lemonade and iced tea, and lawn games (croquet, horseshoes, badminton). Daytime weddings mean less expensive venue fees and guests will eat and drink less than in the evening, cutting catering and bar costs.

- Play around with themes and concepts to avoid a sit-down dinner. A family style Italian meal, barbecue hot off the smoker, or an East Coast-inspired clambake are fun ideas for couples' looking for a wallet-friendly alternative to a formal reception.

- Plan a backyard wedding to save on venue costs, but review the considerations mentioned earlier in this chapter. The home will need to accommodate your guests, their vehicles, your caterer, a bar, a dance floor, DJ, and more. Also, consider your proximity to neighbors, who won't want to be kept up late at night with the sound of loud music and voices.

- Get creative and utilize a facility that is accessible to you for a low cost, such as your neighborhood's community center, country club's clubhouse, local library, public garden, local college or university, or zoo. If you think a venue has a nice ambiance, it doesn't hurt to inquire about hosting an event there.

- Get a permit to have your wedding in a local park. Fees will probably be very low. Consider whether the venue provides ample seating, electrical outlets for your entertainment, restrooms, free parking, etc.

- Lighting can make an average venue seem romantic, intimate and beautiful instantly. Add candles or strings of white lights, or inquire about renting small and inexpensive spotlights or lanterns. Things like tea lights and pillar candles can be purchase very cheaply and in bulk.

## Real Couples' Weddings

- "We planned to get married in an exclusive beach community in Southern California, and it never occurred to us that the local country club where our family friends lived would be a budget-friendly venue. Turns out, it is the best deal in town! They provided great food and had minimal noise restrictions, unlike many other venues we looked into. Find a yacht club or country club and see if someone you know is a member and can get you an inexpensive rental fee."
~ Marni L., Corona, CA

- "Be sure to check whether you have to use a reception venue's vendor list, or whether it is just a suggestion. It's a big money-saver to bring in your own rental company, caterer and bartender, many times. All-inclusive wedding packages seem low-stress, but they're typically much more expensive than if you price out each piece yourself."
~ Linda S., Burlington, VT

## HORS D'OEUVRES

At receptions where a full meal is to be served, hors d'oeuvres may be offered to guests during the first hour of the reception. However, at a tea or cocktail reception, hors d'oeuvres will be the main course. Having an hors d'oeuvres-heavy cocktail hour, instead of a sit-down dinner, can save thousands on catering.

Options: There are many options for hors d'oeuvres, depending on the formality and theme of your reception. Popular items are foods that can easily be picked up and eaten with one hand. Hors d'oeuvres may be set out on tables "buffet style" for guests to help themselves, or they may be passed around on trays by waiters and waitresses.

Things to Consider: When selecting hors d'oeuvres for your reception, consider whether heating or refrigeration will be available and choose your food accordingly. When planning your menu, consider the time of day. You should select lighter hors d'oeuvres for a midday reception and heavier hors d'oeuvres for an evening reception. Coordinate the food you serve with your theme and season; for instance, mini quesadillas and beef canapes for a Mexican fiesta-themed wedding or butternut squash soup shooters for a fall event.

Price Range: $3 - $20 per person

## Ideas to Save Money

▶ Compare at least three caterers; there is a wide price range between caterers for the same food. Many times, a restaurant or company that doesn't specialize in wedding catering can save money from hiring a traditional wedding caterer.

▶ Avoid serving hors d'oeuvres that are labor intensive or that require expensive ingredients or cooling systems. For instance, skip the sushi bar.

▶ Avoid a buffet table of hors d'oeuvres, which prompts guests to eat more than they normally would, or else have waiters put out a portion of the food and only restock the buffet when one item gets low.

▶ Ask if you can take one of the hors d'oeuvres off the menu to lower the price. Be aware that if you are having an hors d'oeurves-only reception, you will need to order more of one of the less expensive menu items to ensure that there is enough food.

## MAIN MEAL

If your reception is going to be at a hotel, restaurant or other facility that provides food, you will need to select a meal to serve your guests. Most of these facilities will have a predetermined menu from which to select your meal. If your reception is going to be in a facility that does not provide food, you will need to hire an outside caterer. The caterer will be responsible for preparing, cooking, and serving the food. The caterer will also be responsible for beverages and for cleaning up after the event. Before signing a contract, make sure you understand all the services the caterer will provide. Your contract should state the amount and type of food and beverages that will be served, the way in which they will be served, the number of servers who will be available, and the cost per food item or person.

**Options:** The main meal can be served either buffet style or as a sit-down meal. It should be chosen according to the time of day, year, and formality of the wedding. Although there are many main dishes to choose from, chicken and beef are the most popular selections for a large event. Ask your facility manager or caterer for their specialty. If you have a special type of food you would like to serve at your reception, select a facility or caterer who specializes in preparing it.

**Things to Consider:** When hiring a caterer, check to see if the location for your reception provides refrigeration and cooking equipment. If not, make sure your caterer is fully self-supported with portable refrigeration and heating equipment. Avoid mayonnaise, cream sauces, or custard fillings if food must go unrefrigerated for any length of time. A competent caterer will prepare much of the food in his or her own kitchen and should provide an adequate staff of cooks, servers, and bartenders.

Ask for references and look at photos from previous parties so you know how the food will be presented; or better yet, visit an event they are catering. A good caterer will set up a food tasting for you. Just be sure to doublecheck if the tasting is free. Some tastings have a small fee. In some instances, caterers will be sneaky and try and charge for the tasting after the fact, if you don't book with them.

**Price Range:** $30 - $150 per person

## Ideas to Save Money

▶ Give only 85 to 95 percent of your final guest count to your caterer or facility manager. Oftentimes, a few guests who have RSVP'd won't show up. Additionally, caterers always provide extra food, in case of an emergency, so no one will go hungry. This is especially true with buffet-style receptions.

▶ Many weddings offer a trio of entree choices: typically, chicken, beef and fish. Serve only chicken to save about $20 a head, but make the dish special, with a citrus glaze or special sauce, for instance.

- Have the reception at a restaurant and have them provide both the food and venue for one price.

- Ask if the caterers you are considering have a minimum for either number of guests served or amount spent. For example, if you are inviting 120 people and your caterer has a 125-person minimum, you will be stuck paying for at least five, and probably more, extra meals. Find a different caterer who better suits your needs if this is the case.

- If offering a buffet meal, have the catering staff serve the food onto guests' plates rather than allowing guests to serve themselves. This will help to regulate the amount of food consumed.

- Consider a brunch or early afternoon wedding so the reception will fall between meals, allowing you to serve inexpensive breakfast food or hors d'oeuvres instead of a full meal.

- Serve the meal family style, where large platters are placed on each table. This gives guests the feeling of a formal sit-down dinner with buffet-style presentation because guests serve themselves. Plus, the food becomes the table centerpieces so you can skip pricey flowers!

- A locally grown or vegetarian menu is typically less expensive than other meal options. Deliciously prepared vegetables, soups, salads or a pasta dish are impressive and tasty. For a vegetarian menu, hire a caterer who specializes in these items, and your guests won't even miss meat.

- Consider a unique and fun menu of less expensive items that go with a theme, such as barbecue, burger sliders and sweet potato fries, fajitas, a pasta station, omelet chef, or picnic food.

### Real Couples' Weddings

- "My fiancée and I went to a tasting with a restaurant that wasn't very experienced with wedding catering. We were surprised when they served us a complete multi-course meal, including several cocktails, at our tasting. We were even more surprised by the $200 bill they sent us after we decided to go with someone else. We refused to pay it, because they never mentioned a fee up-front, but other couples should watch out for food tastings that seem too good to be true."
  ~ Matt P., Westport, CT

▶ "We hired a paella chef who prepped and cooked huge pans of paella with chicken and seafood right at our reception. The price was right, and I could hear guests commenting on the delicious smell when we entered the courtyard."

~ Grace J., Santa Fe, NM

▶ "What makes Mediterranean cuisine so tasty are fresh vegetables and lots of spices — things that aren't expensive! We had our wedding catered by a local Greek restaurant, and we got literally three times as much food of all different varieties — dips, sides, entrees, — for our money. Everything was unique and delicious and the restaurant charged us less because they aren't a 'wedding caterer.'"

~ Chelsea Y., San Francisco, CA

## LIQUOR/BEVERAGES

Prices for liquor and beverages vary greatly, depending on the amount and brand of alcohol served. Couples can decide to have an alcohol-free wedding or limit the bar to a portion of the event to save money. Traditionally, at least champagne or sparkling cider should be served to toast the couple.

Options: White and red wines, scotch, vodka, gin, rum, and beer are the most popular alcoholic beverages. Soda, lemonade and iced tea are popular nonalcoholic beverages at receptions. And of course, don't forget coffee or tea.

There are a number of options and variations for serving alcoholic beverages: a full open bar where you pay for your guests to drink as much as they wish; an open bar for the first hour, followed by a cash bar where guests pay for their own drinks; beer and wine only; cash bar only; nonalcoholic beverages only; or any combination.

Things to Consider: If you plan to serve alcoholic beverages at a reception site that does not provide liquor, make sure your caterer has a license to serve alcohol and that your reception site allows alcoholic beverages. If you plan to order your own alcohol, do so three or four weeks before the event. If you plan to have a no-host or cash bar, notify; your guests so they know to bring cash with them. A simple line that says "No-Host Bar" on the reception card should suffice.

In selecting the type of alcohol to serve, consider the age and preference of your guests, the type of food that will be served, and the time of day your guests will be drinking. Never serve liquor without some type of food.

On the average, you should assume one drink per person, per hour at the reception. If you are hosting an open bar at a hotel or restaurant, ask the catering manager how they charge for liquor: by consumption or by number of bottles opened. Get this in writing and ask for a full consumption report after the event.

Lastly, it is not uncommon for the hosts of a party to be held legally responsible for the conduct and safety of their guests. Keep this in mind when planning the quantity and type of beverages to serve. Also, be sure to remind your bartenders not to serve alcohol to minors.

Use the following chart to plan your beverage needs:

| Beverages | Amount based on 100 guests |
| --- | --- |
| Bourbon | 3 Fifths |
| Gin | 3 Fifths |
| Rum | 2 Fifths |
| Scotch | 4 Quarts |
| Vodka | 5 Quarts |
| White Wine | 2 Cases |
| Red Wine | 1 Case |
| Champagne | 3 Cases |
| Other | 2 Cases each: Club Soda, Seltzer Water, Tonic Water, Ginger Ale, Cola, Beer |

Price Range: $8 - $60 per person

## Ideas to Save Money

▶ To keep beverage costs down, serve only beer and wine, or nonalcoholic drinks only, such as a gourmet coffee and tea bar.

▶ For the toast, pour champagne only for those guests who ask for it. Many people will make a toast with whatever they are currently drinking. Likewise, many people don't drink champagne and their toasting pours will go to waste.

▶ Serve prosecco or cava, two types of sparkling wine that look and taste likes champagne, but are cheaper. Or consider serving sparkling cider in place of champagne.

▶ If some guests won't be drinking alcohol (children, non-drinkers, religious guests), give your caterer or venue a "bar count" instead of a full head count. That way, you won't be charged for alcohol for the guests who you know won't indulge.

▶ Buy cases of inexpensive wine or liquor from the grocery store or warehouse stores like Costco. Ask if you can return any bottles you don't open.

▶ If you don't want your guests to know you've chosen an inexpensive brand of wine, decanter the wine and keep the full bottles behind the bar, or affix a personalized label.

▶ For a fiesta-themed wedding, rent an inexpensive margarita machine. They run about $200; you simply provide the ice, tequila and margarita mix, which can be bought inexpensively from a liquor or grocery store.

▶ Host alcoholic beverages for the first hour, then go to a cash bar. Or host beer, wine, and soft drinks only and have mixed drinks available on a cash basis.

▶ Omit waiters and waitresses. People tend to drink almost twice as much if there are waiters and waitresses constantly asking them if they would like another drink and then bringing drinks to them.

▶ Serve one personalized drink instead of a full liquor selection. Choose something meaningful to you as a couple — the cocktail you drank on your first date, for example. Include a sign at the bar that tells the story of your special drink. You might even include the recipe and a special glass as a favor for guests.

▶ Put a cap on alcohol consumption. Tell your caterer or bartender to keep track of the amount consumed and stop serving at a set amount of money you decide on ahead of time. At that point, you can give the go-ahead to continue serving or to stop serving alcoholic beverages. Get this written into your contract.

▶ "Use all your connections to save money. In graduate school, I organized most of our social events, so I had a friendly relationship with a liquor store owner who provided the kegs for our parties and tailgates. I called him about alcohol for my wedding, and he ended up giving me two free beer kegs, plus the taps and tubs. We kept them behind the bar so the reception didn't look like a house party."
~ Steve H., Louisville, KY

▶ "Don't tell anyone, but we bought cases of Two Buck Chuck from Trader Joe's, peeled off the labels, and glued on our own personalized labels!"
~ Andrea S., Northbrook, IL

▶ "We had Izze sodas and sparkling water with lemon or lime slices, which was colorful, refreshing and much less inexpensive than having cocktails. We're not big drinkers and neither are most of our friends. We had the casual picnic feel we wanted without spending thousands on alcohol."
~ Olivia B., Houston, TX

## BARTENDING/BAR SETUP FEE

Some reception sites and caterers charge an extra fee for bartending and for setting up the bar.

Price Range:  $75 - $500

**Ideas to Save Money** 💲

▶ The bartending fee could be and often is waived if you meet a minimum requirement on beverages consumed. Try to negotiate this with your caterer prior to hiring him or her.

## CORKAGE FEE

Many reception sites and caterers make money by marking up the food and alcohol they sell. You may wish to provide your own alcohol for several reasons. First, it is more cost effective. Second, you may want to serve an exotic wine or champagne that the reception site or caterer does not offer. In either case, and if your reception site or caterer allows it, be prepared to pay a corkage fee. This is the fee for each bottle brought into the reception site and opened by a member of their staff.

Things to Consider: You need to consider whether the expenses saved after paying the corkage fee justifies the hassle of bringing in your own alcohol.

Price Range: $5 - $20 per bottle

### Ideas to Save Money

▶ Purchase alcohol from a store that allows you to return any unopened bottles. Always get a count of what was opened and what was not finished.

### Real Couples' Weddings

▶ "We bought handles of liquor and magnums of wine from Sam's Club to save money and avoid unneccessary corkage fees.
~ Brittany B., Oklahoma City, OK


## FEE TO POUR COFFEE

In addition to corkage and cake-cutting fees, some facilities also charge extra to pour coffee with the wedding cake.

Things to Consider: Again, when comparing the cost of various reception sites, don't forget to add up all the extra miscellaneous costs, such as the fee for pouring coffee.

Price Range: $0.25 - $1 per person


## SERVICE PROVIDERS' MEALS

Things to Consider: It is considered a courtesy to feed your photographer, videographer, and any other service providers at the reception. Check options and prices with your caterer or reception site manager.

Make sure you allocate a place for your service providers to eat. You may want them to eat with your guests, or you may prefer setting a place outside the main room for them to eat. Your service providers may be more comfortable with the latter.

Price Range: $10 - $30 per person

## Ideas to Save Money

▶ If the meal is a buffet, there should be enough food left after all your guests have been served for your service providers to eat. Tell them they are welcome to eat after all your guests have been served. Be sure to discuss this with your catering manager.

▶ You don't need to feed your service providers the same meal as your guests. You can order sandwiches or another less expensive meal for them.

## Real Couples' Weddings

▶ "A great tip: Because photographers typically get to eat the same food as the wedding guests, our photographer had a wealth of knowledge about caterers — whose food was great or just average, the most attractive setups, and other insider information."
~ Vanessa S., St. Louis, MI

## GRATUITY

It is customary to pay a gratuity to your caterer. This is usually an amount that is pre-set and detailed in the contract. Be sure to ask whether a caterer charges both gratuity and labor fees, which can add up to thousands of dollars.

Price Range: 15 - 25 percent of total food and beverage bill

## Ideas to Save Money

▶ Ask about these costs up-front and select your caterer or reception site accordingly.

## PARTY FAVORS

Party favors are gift items given to your guests as mementos of your wedding. They are typically personalized with your names and wedding date or coordinate with the theme of your event.

**Options:** Frames, candles, CDs of music, jams and jellies, flower seeds, chocolates, or fine candy are all popular wedding favors. Wine or champagne bottles marked with the bride and groom's names and wedding date on a personalized label are also popular. These come in different sizes and can be purchased by the case.

**Things to Consider:** Personalized favors need to be ordered several weeks in advance.

**Price Range:** $1 - $15 per person

### Ideas to Save Money

▶ Unfortunately, many guests will leave favors behind, unless the favor is immediately edible. Many couples on a budget skip favors all together.

▶ Burning your own CDs of your favorite music can be an inexpensive gift; however, consider the size of your guest list and copyright laws.

▶ If you didn't rent the vases, have guests take centerpieces or floral decorations home as gifts.

## ONLINE PHOTO ALBUM

Skip the disposable cameras; these days, most guests will bring their own digital cameras, which take much sharper, clearer photos than their cardboard counterparts, anyhow. Create an online photo album where guests can go to upload their digital photos for all to see.

**Options:** There are many websites that allow you to create an online, shareable photo gallery, including Flickr, Snapfish, Picasa and Photobucket. Standard space is free, or you can purchase increased storage space for just $5 to $25 per year. Create a URL, login and password for your wedding gallery. Then, hand out small cards with this information at your wedding, or email the information to all your guests after the wedding so everyone can upload the photos they took.

Price Range: $0 - $25

## ROSE PETALS/RICE

Rose petals or rice are traditionally tossed over the bride and groom as they leave the church after the ceremony or when they leave the reception to symbolize happiness, beauty, and prosperity.

Options: Rose petals, rice, sparklers or confetti are often used. You may also want to use grass or flower seeds, which do not need to be cleaned up if tossed over a grassy area.

Things to Consider: Some venues do not allow rose petals, which can be slippery, or confetti, which needs to be cleaned up. Sparklers are also a popular option that look beautiful in photos, although some venues do not allow them because they could be a smoke or fire hazard. Ask about your venue's policy.

Price Range: $0.35 - $2 per person

## GIFT ATTENDANT

The gift attendant is responsible for watching over your gifts during the reception so that no one walks away with them. Do not have a friend or family member take on this duty as he or she would not enjoy the reception. The gift attendant should also be responsible for transporting your gifts from the reception site to your car or bridal suite.

Things to Consider: A gift attendant is only necessary only if your reception is held in a public area such as a hotel, public beach or outside garden where strangers may be walking by.

Price Range: $20 - $100

▶ If you hire a wedding planner for the day of your event, he or she can act of the gift attendant. Wedding party members can also help move gifts.

## PARKING FEE/VALET SERVICES

Options: Many reception sites charge for parking. It is customary, although not necessary, for the host of the wedding to pay this charge. At a home reception, you should consider hiring a professional, insured valet service. You can also arrange for guests to park at a nearby school or church and rent a bus or van to shuttle guests to the reception site.

Price Range:  $3 - $15 per car

▶ Let your guests pay their own parking fees or ask them to carpool.

▶ Find a venue that includes a parking lot to accommodate your guest list in their rental package.

**HORS D'OEUVRES:**

_____

_____

_____

_____

**SALADS/APPETIZERS:**

_____

_____

_____

**SOUPS:**

_____

_____

**MAIN ENTREE:**

_____

_____

_____

_____

_____

**DESSERTS:**

_____

_____

_____

**WEDDING CAKE:**

_____

_____

_____

_____

## RECEPTION SITE COMPARISON CHART

| Questions | POSSIBILITY 1 |
|---|---|
| What is the name of the reception site? | |
| What is the website and e-mail of the reception site? | |
| What is the address of the reception site? | |
| What is the name and phone number of my contact person? | |
| What dates and times are available? | |
| What is the maximum number of guests for a seated reception? | |
| What is the maximum number of guests for a cocktail reception? | |
| What is the reception site fee? | |
| What is the price range for a seated lunch? | |
| What is the price range for a buffet lunch? | |
| What is the price range for a seated dinner? | |
| What is the price range for a buffet dinner? | |
| What is the corkage fee? | |
| What is the cake-cutting fee? | |
| What is the ratio of servers to guests? | |
| How much time will be allotted for my reception? | |
| What music restrictions are there, if any? | |

| POSSIBILITY 2 | POSSIBILITY 3 |
|---|---|
|  |  |
|  |  |
|  |  |
|  |  |
|  |  |
|  |  |
|  |  |
|  |  |
|  |  |
|  |  |
|  |  |
|  |  |
|  |  |
|  |  |
|  |  |
|  |  |
|  |  |

| Questions | POSSIBILITY 1 |
|---|---|
| What alcohol restrictions are there, if any? | |
| Are there any restrictions for rice or rose petal tossing? | |
| What room and table decorations are available? | |
| Is a changing room available? | |
| Is there handicap accessibility? | |
| Is a dance floor included in the site fee? | |
| Are tables, chairs, and linens included in the site fee? | |
| Are outside caterers allowed? | |
| Are kitchen facilities available for outside caterers? | |
| Does the facility have full liability insurance? | |
| What perks or giveaways are offered? | |
| How many parking spaces are available for my wedding party? | |
| How many parking spaces are available for my guests? | |
| What is the cost for parking, if any? | |
| What is the cost for sleeping rooms, if available? | |
| What is the payment policy? | |
| What is the cancellation policy? | |

| POSSIBILITY 2 | POSSIBILITY 3 |
|---|---|
| | |
| | |
| | |
| | |
| | |
| | |
| | |
| | |
| | |
| | |
| | |
| | |
| | |
| | |
| | |
| | |

## RECEPTION SITE INFORMATION SHEET

**RECEPTION SITE:**

Site Coordinator: _____ Cost: _____

Website: _____

E-mail: _____

Phone: _____ Fax: _____

Address: _____

City: _____ State: _____ Zip: _____

Name of Room: _____ Room Capacity: _____

Date Confirmed: _____ Confirm Head Count By: _____

Beginning Time: _____ Ending Time: _____

Cocktails/Hors d'Oeuvres Time: _____ Meal Time: _____

Color of Linens: _____ Color of Napkins: _____

Total Cost: _____

Deposit: _____ Date: _____

Balance: _____ Date Due: _____

Cancellation Policy: _____

**EQUIPMENT INCLUDES:**

❑ Tables ❑ Chairs ❑ Linens ❑ Tableware
❑ Bar ware ❑ Heaters ❑ Electric Outlet ❑ Musical Instruments

**SERVICE INCLUDES:**

❑ Waiters ❑ Bartenders ❑ Valet ❑ Main Meal
❑ Clean Up ❑ Setup ❑ Security ❑ Free Parking

## CATERER:

Contact Person: _____   Cost Per Person: _____

Website: _____

E-mail: _____

Phone: _____   Fax: _____

Address: _____

City: _____   State: _____   Zip: _____

Confirmed Date: _____   Confirm Head Count By: _____

Arrival Time: _____   Departure Time: _____

Cocktails/Hors d'Oeuvres Time: ____   Meal Time: _____

Color of Linens: _____   Color of Napkins: _____

Total Cost: _____

Deposit: _____   Date: _____

Balance: _____   Date Due: _____

Cancellation Policy: _____

## EQUIPMENT INCLUDES:

❏ Tables      ❏ Chairs      ❏ Linens      ❏ Tableware
❏ Bar ware    ❏ Heaters     ❏ Lighting    ❏ Candles

## SERVICE INCLUDES:

❏ Waiters     ❏ Bartenders       ❏ Setup         ❏ Clean Up
❏ Security    ❏ Hors d'Oeuvres   ❏ Buffet Meal   ❏ Seated Meal
❏ Cocktails   ❏ Champagne        ❏ Wine          ❏ Beer
❏ Punch       ❏ Soft Drinks      ❏ Coffee/Tea    ❏ Cake

## TABLE SEATING ARRANGEMENTS

*Complete this form only after finalizing your guest list.*

| Head Table | Bride's Family Table | Groom's Family Table |
|---|---|---|
| _____ | _____ | _____ |
| _____ | _____ | _____ |
| _____ | _____ | _____ |
| _____ | _____ | _____ |
| _____ | _____ | _____ |
| _____ | _____ | _____ |
| _____ | _____ | _____ |
| _____ | _____ | _____ |
| • Table _____ | • Table _____ | • Table _____ |
| _____ | _____ | _____ |
| _____ | _____ | _____ |
| _____ | _____ | _____ |
| _____ | _____ | _____ |
| _____ | _____ | _____ |
| _____ | _____ | _____ |
| _____ | _____ | _____ |
| _____ | _____ | _____ |
| • Table _____ | • Table _____ | • Table _____ |
| _____ | _____ | _____ |
| _____ | _____ | _____ |
| _____ | _____ | _____ |
| _____ | _____ | _____ |
| _____ | _____ | _____ |
| _____ | _____ | _____ |
| _____ | _____ | _____ |

Liquor Retailer: _____ Date Ordered: _____

Contact: _____ Phone: _____

Website: _____

E-mail: _____

Address: _____

City: _____ State: _____ Zip: _____

Cost: _____

Delivered By: _____ Delivery Date: _____

| Type of Liquor | # of Bottles | Price |
| --- | --- | --- |
| | | |
| | | |
| | | |
| | | |
| | | |
| | | |
| | | |
| | | |
| | | |
| | | |
| | | |
| | | |
| | | |
| | | |
| | | |

# CATERER COMPARISON CHART

| Questions | POSSIBILITY 1 |
|---|---|
| What is the name of the caterer? | |
| What is the website and e-mail of the caterer? | |
| What is the address of the caterer? | |
| What is the name and phone number of my contact person? | |
| How many years have you been in business? | |
| What percentage of your business is dedicated to receptions? | |
| Do you have liability insurance/license to serve alcohol? | |
| When is the final head-count needed? | |
| What is your ratio of servers to guests? | |
| How do your servers dress for wedding receptions? | |
| Price range for a seated lunch/buffet lunch? | |
| Price range for a seated/buffet dinner? | |
| How much gratuity is expected? | |
| What is your cake-cutting fee? | |
| What is your bartending fee? | |
| What is your fee to clean up after the reception? | |
| What is your payment/cancellation policy? | |

| POSSIBILITY 2 | POSSIBILITY 3 |
|---|---|
|  |  |
|  |  |
|  |  |
|  |  |
|  |  |
|  |  |
|  |  |
|  |  |
|  |  |
|  |  |
|  |  |
|  |  |
|  |  |
|  |  |
|  |  |
|  |  |

# WEDDING PLANNING NOTES

# Kate & Jordan

Total Spent: $8,400

July 25, 2009 • Vashon Island, Washington • 180 guests
Photography by Garrett Grove, http://groveweddings.com

## Budget Breakdown

| | | | | |
|---|---|---|---|---|
| Attire | $350 | Bar | $0 |
| Stationery | $100 | Music | $50 |
| Ceremony & Reception Site | $1,800 | Bakery | N/A |
| | | Flowers | $600 |
| Photography | $1,000 | Décor & Rental Items | $1,000 |
| Videography | N/A | Miscellaneous | $700 |
| Food | $2,800 | **Total** | $8,400 |

Friends and family at Kate and Jordan's wedding were treated to a happy-go-lucky day complete with organic Sno-Kones and cotton candy, all-you-can-eat barbecue, an antique organ, Bocce ball, badminton, and croquet, and an inflatable bounce house for both adults and kids to enjoy. The romantic lavender fields of Washington's Fox Farm and a sunny summer day set the backdrop for the event, which Kate explained by saying, "We love summer days in Seattle lounging around at the park on Lake Washington with all our friends. We wanted to take the carefree feeling of those days and translate them into our perfect wedding!"

## FROM THE BRIDE

It was important to us to keep our costs down, because while we wanted our wedding to be special, we knew that it was just the beginning of a very exciting journey, not the destination. We didn't want to accrue any debt that we would bring into our new marriage. Since I am a teacher and my husband is in grad school, that left us with only the $8,000 my mom was contributing to the big day. To be honest, when we started planning we didn't know that $8,000 was a "limited" budget. It seemed like a ton of money to us, and we even felt a little guilty about spending so much money on one day!

It was really important to us that the wedding accurately represented us as a couple. The first thing we did was decide on a theme, or feel. We wanted it to feel like the perfect day at the park, so that was what we kept in mind as we planned. My husband is from a small island outside of Seattle and we were able to find a beautiful lavender farm that did weddings. We saved money by choosing one location for both our ceremony and reception and by choosing a location that was beautiful all by itself. It didn't need many decorations, because it was naturally breathtaking.

## DÉCOR

We wanted our day to be memorable and unique even though we were on a budget, so we tried to think of details that were cost-effective but also special. For instance, we bought an antique organ for the ceremony music for just $50 from a couple we found on Craigslist. They had played the same one at their wedding 32 years earlier! We hung a vintage chandelier that we got for $20 from a salvage store from the tree we were married under. The flower girls wore handmade tutus. We rented a cotton candy machine and ordered organic raspberry cotton candy from an online vendor, which we served during the reception. We also rented a Sno-Kone machine and purchased organic syrups in lychee, ginger ale, and grapefruit flavors and served those before the ceremony, when guests first arrived. The Sno-Kones and cotton candy were definitely a hit! It was really hot out, so the Sno-Kones were a refreshing life-saver. We

also rented a bounce house and set up lawn games throughout the sprawling venue. Sapling favors in burlap sacks created a natural carbon offset for all the traveling guests had to do to get to the island. We even rode away on our own red scooter, named Ruby Scoot, decorated by our friends.

We had a lot of people who told us throughout our engagement that they would like to help, and we took them up on it! Friends and family made pies that we arranged on wood

stumps cut from a neighbors' fallen tree. The groom's childhood friend officiated the ceremony and a team of family and friends did all the setup and clean up. One of my dearest friends took on the job of day-of coordinator. One of the bridesmaids did all of our hair. A friend of ours is an incredible wedding photographer and he gave us a discount.

## ATTIRE

I got my dress from J. Crew. I signed up for their email list and waited to order my dress until I received an online coupon. J. Crew also has a teacher discount, which I was able to apply on top of the coupon. Businesses often give discounts to civil service, military, nurses, and teachers, and brides who don't fall under these categories themselves might have a family member who could get them the discount. My husband got his suit at H&M, which was cheaper than renting a tux and looked better.

It was important to us that we kept things affordable for our bridal party, as well. We wanted being a part of our wedding to be an honor, not a burden. We asked the groomsmen to wear matching ties that we bought them, but told them they could wear khaki pants and white shirts that they already owned.

I didn't pick colors for our day until I found bridesmaids' dresses on sale. They were also from J. Crew and, because I wasn't attached to a color, we were able to choose dresses that were on clearance and use my teacher discount.

### FLOWERS

The only flowers we ended up adding for ambience were from a local farmer's market. My in-laws picked them up the day before the wedding and placed them in antique mason jars I got from Craigslist. I wasn't picky about the variety of flower, so

they just bought everything that was beautiful and affordable. They were able to negotiate with vendors because they got there when the market was shutting down. The flowers in the mason jars were placed on vintage linens that I gathered from antique and thrift stores.

## FOOD

We contacted local barbecue restaurants to find out if they catered. Since barbecue food isn't typical wedding food, it didn't have the wedding price tag. We were able to treat our guests to all-they-could-eat ribs, beef brisket, pulled pork, BBQ chicken, coleslaw, potato salad and cornbread from Jasper's BBQ, who cater for the Seahawks and Microsoft, for $13 a person. They served the food right off the smoker, which was so much fun and went with our theme. Brides should think of non-wedding food in order to save money.

## PHOTOGRAPHY

Of all the things we spent money on, the most important was definitely the photographer. His pictures are absolutely incredible and we will have them forever. There are many moments he captured that we missed and I am so grateful for his pictures. This is the one area where I would encourage brides to splurge.

## ADVICE

Honestly, we spent so much time planning that we thought we would be really worried about details the day of. It turned out we were less concerned with all

the little details and more concerned about spending time with all the people who were there. There was a lot for people to do, and it all felt very natural and laid-back. One of our favorite moments was when we got a chance to bounce with each other in the bounce house right after the ceremony.

My best advice would be for brides to choose a theme for their wedding and then think of special, unique details that go with it. It is the little details that really make it special and those details don't usually come with big price tags.

The most unexpected event on our wedding day was actually after the wedding was over. We went back to the cabin we had rented, but it was only 7 p.m., and we were still really amped up from such an amazing day. We realized that all our friends and family were on the same island for probably the only time in our lives and we wanted to be with them! We quickly called our friends and found out they had met up at Dockton, a local beach, to go swimming. We hopped on our "getaway scooter" and headed over to meet them. We decided to stay in our wedding attire because this was, after all, the only day we got to wear it! We all ended up laughing and talking on a dock from Jordan's childhood as we watched the sunset. It felt so good to end our day with a small group of friends who really supported and loved each other. We still can't believe how special it was to have everyone we loved in one place at one time.

# Music

MUSIC IS A MAJOR PART OF YOUR wedding ceremony and reception. Music helps set the tone and mood of each portion of the day, whether you want guests quietly watching the processional, mingling and enjoying cocktails, or having a blast on the dance floor.

## CEREMONY MUSIC

Ceremony music is the music played during the prelude, processional, ceremony, recessional, and postlude. Prelude music is played while guests are being seated, 15 to 30 minutes before the ceremony begins. Processional music is played as the wedding party enters the ceremony site. Recessional music is played as the wedding party leaves the ceremony site. Postlude music is played while the guests leave the ceremony site.

Options: The most traditional musical instrument for wedding ceremonies is the organ. But guitars, pianos, flutes, harps, and violins are also popular.

Things to Consider: Music may or may not be included as part of the ceremony site fee. Be sure to check with your ceremony site about restrictions pertaining to music and the availability of musical instruments for your use.

Discuss the selection of ceremony music with your officiant and musicians. Make sure the musicians know how to play the selections you request. Be aware that sheet music isn't written for instruments like the organ, so give your musicians plenty of heads up if you want them to learn a nontraditional song.

When selecting ceremony music, keep in mind the formality of your wedding, your religious affiliation, and the length of the ceremony. Also consider the location and time of day. If the ceremony is outside where there may be other noises such as traffic, wind, or people's voices, or if a large number of guests will be attending your ceremony, consider having the music, your officiant, and your vows amplified.

Price Range: $100 - $900

## Ideas to Save Money

▶ Hire student musicians from your local university or high school. Contact the directors of their music programs and have them help you find the right musicians for your event, or post a flyer with the details of what you need and when on the school's bulletin boards.

▶ Ask a talented friend to sing or play at your ceremony; he or she will be honored.

▶ If you're planning to hire a band for your reception, consider hiring a scaled-down version of the same band to play at your ceremony, such as a trio of flute, guitar, and vocals. This could enable you to negotiate a "package" price.

▶ If you're planning to hire a DJ for your reception, consider asking him or her to play pre-recorded music during your ceremony.

## Real Couples' Weddings

▶ "We got married in the church at Kevin's high school, so we had several members of the school's marching band play our ceremony music. It sounded great, and it was free!"
~ Lisa E., Albany, NY

## RECEPTION MUSIC

Special songs will make your reception unique. When you select music for your reception, keep in mind the age and musical preference of your guests, your budget, and any restrictions that the reception site may have.

**Options:** You need to find a reliable DJ, band, or combination of instruments and vocalists who will play the type of music you want and keep guests feeling upbeat all night. They should have experience performing at wedding receptions so they understand the flow of the event and can hopefully act as your master of ceremonies.

**Things to Consider:** If you want your musician to be your MC, make sure he or she has a complete timeline for your reception in order to announce the various events such as the toasts, first dance, and cutting of the cake.

If you need a large variety of music to satisfy all your guests, consider hiring a DJ. Make sure you give him or her a list of the songs you want played at your reception and the sequence in which you want them played. You may also want to provide a "Do Not Play" list of songs you don't want the DJ to play, even if they are requested. Consider the equipment your DJ will need. Some DJs travel with their amps and speakers and some do not. If that is the case, your venue will need to supply equipment or you will need to rent it.

If you choose a live band, consider watching your musicians perform at another event before booking their services. You should provide them with a few modern songs you would like at your reception and see if they are able to play them. You should also find out if you need to provide prerecorded music to play while the musicians take a break during the reception.

You should consider whether you want to hire a regular DJ or an entertainer — a DJ who can also provide things like disco dance lessons for the crowd or a light show. Some DJs interact with the crowd much more than others. Decide which type of DJ you want.

Be sure to check with your reception venue about any music restrictions. Some venues located in residential areas, for instance, may have a rule that music has to be off by 10 p.m. Receptions held on Sunday nights may have noise and music restrictions as well. Consider this when choosing a venue.

**Price Range:** $500 - $5,000

▶ Check the music department of local colleges and universities for names of student musicians and DJs. You may be able to hire a student for a fraction of the price of a professional musician or DJ.

▶ Book on an off-peak night. DJs and bands may charge 10 to 20 percent more for a Saturday night wedding. Additionally, booking a DJ near the holidays or on New Year's Eve can nearly double the price!

▶ Bands and musicians are typically much more expensive than DJs. If you do hire a band, consider a smaller group of musicians, which will cost less and means having to give gratuity to fewer people. A good three-piece band can sound like many more musicians with the right instruments and acoustics. Just be sure to consider the size of your venue. You won't want a tiny band echoing through a huge banquet hall.

▶ A word to the wise regarding "iPod weddings" — for a very small, intimate backyard wedding, playing a preset playlist of music may be acceptable. However, consider that you will need to rent speakers and a microphone, provide enough power for the duration of the event, and be sure to have a backup CD. You will also need a guest or vendor who can man the iPod or mp3 player and make sure it is started and stopped at the right times and that no unruly guests change the song. An iPod wedding is also risky in that if something goes wrong with the equipment you could be left without any musical entertainment at all. If you do decide to forego professional music in favor of a playlist and speakers, be sure to standardize the volume and crossfade the tracks on your mp3 player so there is no dead air between songs.

## Real Couples' Weddings

▶ "Finding a DJ who fits your style is so important. We've been to weddings where the DJ talked throughout the reception, acting like he knew the couple personally, and we didn't want that. We found a DJ who let us peek in on another wedding he did to be sure he was our style. It showed that he was confident and wanted us to have the right person."
~ Fiona D., San Francisco, CA

## CEREMONY MUSIC SELECTIONS

*Make a copy of this form and give it to your musicians.*

| When | Selection | Composer | Played By |
|------|-----------|----------|-----------|
| Prelude 1 | | | |
| Prelude 2 | | | |
| Prelude 3 | | | |
| Processional | | | |
| Bride's Processional | | | |
| Ceremony 1 | | | |
| Ceremony 2 | | | |
| Ceremony 3 | | | |
| Recessional | | | |
| Postlude | | | |
| Other: | | | |
| Other: | | | |
| Other: | | | |
| Other: | | | |
| Other: | | | |
| Other: | | | |
| Other: | | | |

## CEREMONY MUSIC COMPARISON CHART

| Questions | POSSIBILITY 1 |
|---|---|
| What is the name of the musician or band? | |
| What is the website and e-mail of the musician or band? | |
| What is the address of the musician or band? | |
| What is the name and phone number of my contact person? | |
| How many years of professional experience do you have? | |
| What percentage of your business is dedicated to weddings? | |
| Are you the person who will perform at my wedding? | |
| What instrument(s) do you play/What type of music do you specialize in? | |
| What are your hourly fees? | |
| What is the cost of a soloist? | |
| What is the cost of a duet? | |
| What is the cost of a trio? | |
| What is the cost of a quartet? | |
| How would you dress for my wedding? | |
| Do you have liability insurance? | |
| Do you have a cordless microphone? | |
| What is your payment/cancellation policy? | |

| POSSIBILITY 2 | POSSIBILITY 3 |
|---|---|
| | |
| | |
| | |
| | |
| | |
| | |
| | |
| | |
| | |
| | |
| | |
| | |
| | |
| | |
| | |
| | |

# RECEPTION MUSIC COMPARISON CHART

| Questions | POSSIBILITY 1 |
|---|---|
| What is the name of the musician? Band? DJ? | |
| What is the website and e-mail of the company? | |
| What is the address of the company? | |
| What is the name and phone number of my contact person? | |
| How many years of professional experience do you have? | |
| What percentage of your business is dedicated to receptions? | |
| How many people are in your band? | |
| What type of music do you specialize in? | |
| What type of sound system do you have? | |
| Can you act as a master of ceremonies? How do you dress? | |
| Can you provide a light show? | |
| Do you have a cordless microphone? | |
| How many breaks do you take? How long are they? | |
| Do you play recorded music during breaks? | |
| Do you have liability insurance? | |
| What are your fees for a 4-hour reception? | |
| What is your cost for each additional hour? | |

| POSSIBILITY 2 | POSSIBILITY 3 |
|---|---|
|  |  |
|  |  |
|  |  |
|  |  |
|  |  |
|  |  |
|  |  |
|  |  |
|  |  |
|  |  |
|  |  |
|  |  |
|  |  |
|  |  |
|  |  |
|  |  |
|  |  |

## RECEPTION MUSIC SELECTIONS

*Make a copy of this form and give it to your musicians.*

| When | Selection | Songwriter | Played By |
|---|---|---|---|
| Receiving Line | | | |
| During Hors d'Oeuvres | | | |
| During Dinner | | | |
| First Dance | | | |
| Second Dance | | | |
| Third Dance | | | |
| Bouquet Toss | | | |
| Garter Removal | | | |
| Cutting of the Cake | | | |
| Last Dance | | | |
| Couple Leaving | | | |
| Other: | | | |
| Other: | | | |
| Other: | | | |
| Other: | | | |
| Other: | | | |
| Other: | | | |

# Bakery

YOUR CAKE MAY BE ORDERED FROM your caterer or from a bakery that specializes in wedding cakes. Ask to see photographs of other wedding cakes your baker has created, and by all means, ask for a tasting! Cakes come in so many shapes, sizes and styles that you can easily find ways to be creative on a budget.

## WEDDING CAKE

Options: When ordering your cake, you will have to decide not only on a flavor, but also on a size, shape, and color. You can choose from one large tier or more, smaller tiers. The cake can be round, square, or heart-shaped. The most common flavors are chocolate, carrot, lemon, and vanilla cake. You can be creative by adding a filling to your cake, such as mousse, custard, ganache or a fruit filling. You may also want to consider having tiers of different flavors.

Icing types and toppings vary the price and look of the cake. Fondant provides a smooth, satiny look and doesn't need refrigeration, making it very popular, although it is one of the most expensive icings and the taste is not always great. Marzipan is a paste made from ground almonds and sugar, which is a better-tasting alternative to fondant. It can also be molded into flowers and other decorations. Ganache and buttercream are also popular icings that are lighter and taste great, although they melt easily and may not be the best choice for outdoor weddings. Sugar gum paste is another type of icing that your baker can use to create figurines, flowers, shapes, and more.

**Things to Consider:** Price, workmanship, quality, and taste vary considerably from baker to baker. In addition to flavor, size, and cost, consider decoration and spoilage (sugar keeps longer than cream frostings). The cake should be beautifully displayed and decorated with flowers or greenery. Make sure the baker, caterer, or reception site manager can provide you with a cake-cutting knife. If not, you will need to purchase or rent one.

If you are saving your top tier, it should be removed before the rest of the cake is cut, wrapped in several layers of plastic wrap or put inside a plastic container, and kept frozen until your anniversary.

**Price Range:** $3 - $12 per piece

## Ideas to Save Money

▶ For recommendations on the beauty and style of a cake, ask your florist or photographer. Usually these two vendors work closely with bakers at weddings and can give good recommendations. For recommendations on taste, ask recent brides who they used and what they thought of the flavor of their cakes. Some very beautiful cakes taste horrible, and vice versa.

▶ Opt for cupcakes, which cost $3 or less each. You can have more than one flavor and many times, the cake-cutting fee will be waived. Sometimes the cupcake baker will rent a cupcake tower or you can DIY the project. There are several simple projects online.

▶ Opt for a less expensive dessert and have only a small one-tier wedding cake to cut. Instead of saving the top tier for your first anniversary (avoid freezer burn!), open a bottle of champagne on that day instead.

▶ Get a custom cake or cupcakes from Costco or a grocery store bakery. Add fresh flowers or your personalized cake topper and the cake will look beautiful. While more unconventional, many brides rave about the taste and customer service at these types of bakeries.

▶ Some bakeries require a deposit on columns and plates; other bakeries use disposable columns and plates, saving you the rental fee and the hassle of returning these items. You can also make your own cake stand. There are many simple, pretty DIY projects online.

▶ Order a small one-tier cake from a professional baker for the cake cutting; then, have servers slice an inexpensive sheet cake in the back and bring it out to guests. They'll never know it's not an expensive baker's cake, and sheet cake is priced as low as 50 cents per slice.

▶ Ask friends and family to have a bake-off for your wedding. Pies, cakes, cupcakes, cookies, and dessert pops (a bite of cake on a stick with a candy coating, similar to a lollipop) are all fairly easy to make, and your loved ones will be honored to help. Remember, the more you get people involved, the more special they will feel!

**Real Couples' Weddings**

▶ "Bridal shows are a great place to find a baker. There is endless cake to try! Every baker and flavor and style is different, so a bridal show is a great place to compare and find a good price."
~ Erin K., Washington, D.C.

## GROOM'S CAKE

The groom's cake is an old Southern tradition whereby a small cake is cut up and distributed to guests in little white boxes engraved with the bride and groom's names. Today, the groom's cake, if offered, is cut and served along with the wedding cake.

Options: Usually a chocolate cake decorated with fruit, the groom's cake is sometimes personalized with the groom's favorite sports team or hobby.

Price Range: $1 - $2 per piece

**Ideas to Save Money**

▶ Because of its cost and the labor involved in cutting and distributing the groom's cake, very few people offer this custom anymore.

▶ "You don't need to adhere to the tradition of ordering an entire cake for the groom. We made a groom's cupcake in the shape of a football. I think the baking pan cost $10."
~ Sara K., Boulder, CO

## CAKE DELIVERY/SETUP FEE

This is the fee charged by bakers to deliver and set up your wedding cake at the reception site. It usually includes a deposit on the cake pillars and plate which will be refunded upon their return to the baker.

Price Range: $40 - $100

**Ideas to Save Money**

▶ Find a baker who doesn't charge setup and delivery fees.

▶ Have a trusted friend or family member get a quick lesson on how to set up your cake. Have him or her pick it up and set it up the day of your wedding, then have the florist decorate the cake and/or cake table with flowers and greenery.

## CAKE-CUTTING FEE

Most reception sites and caterers charge a fee for each slice of cake they cut if the cake is brought in from an outside bakery. This fee will probably shock you. It is simply their way of enticing you to order the cake through them. Unfortunately, many caterers will not allow a member of your party to cut the cake.

Price Range: $1 - $3 per person

**Ideas to Save Money**

▶ Many hotels and restaurants include a dessert in the cost of their meal packages. If you forego this dessert and substitute your cake as the dessert, they may be willing to waive the cake-cutting fee. Be sure to ask them.

▶ "We got around the $2 per person cake-cutting fee, which we found outrageous, by serving cupcakes. Just make sure this is fine with your caterer."

~ Crystal L., Minneapolis, MN

## CAKE TOPPER

The bride's cake is often topped with some sort of decoration. Bells, love birds, a bridal couple, your initials or two wedding rings are popular choices and can be saved as mementos of your wedding day.

Things to Consider: Some porcelain and heavy cake toppers need to be anchored down into the cake. Talk to your baker once you choose your cake topper.

Price Range: $10 - $150

**Ideas to Save Money** 💲

▶ Borrow a cake top from a friend or a family member as "something borrowed," an age-old wedding tradition.

▶ Shop for inexpensive sign letters at a hardware or home improvement store. Paint or decorate them and use them as your initials atop your cake.

▶ Have your florist set aside a few large blooms to use as a cake topper.

▶ Make your own cake topper! This can be a fun, quick DIY project that can be redone as many times as needed until you get it right. Peruse an arts and crafts store to get ideas and buy supplies, such as styrofoam, wooden doll bodies, paint, and more.

▶ "Michaels and other crafts stores are a treasure trove of fun and creative ideas! I found little mushrooms, butterflies and hummingbirds that made perfect cake toppers, for about $12. They were perfect with our outdoor wedding and woodsy setting."
   ~ Tara H., Gallatin, TN

## CAKE KNIFE/TOASTING GLASSES

Your cake knife and toasting glasses can be rented, purchased or borrowed. The bride uses the cake knife to cut the first two slices of the wedding cake with the groom's hand placed over hers. The groom feeds the bride first. Then the bride feeds the groom.

You will use toasting glasses to toast each other after cutting the cake. They are usually decorated with ribbons or flowers and kept near the cake. This tradition makes beautiful wedding photographs.

**Things to Consider:** Consider having your initials and wedding date engraved on your wedding knife as a memento. Consider purchasing crystal or silver toasting glasses as a keepsake of your wedding.

**Price Range:** $15 - $120 for knife; $10 - $100 for toasting glasses

**Ideas to Save Money**

▶ Use the reception facility's glasses and knife, and decorate them with flowers or ribbon.

▶ Purchasing a cake knife and glass set from a bridal retailer will be much more expensive than using a regular set of champagne flutes and a cake cutting set. Look for pretty items on sale at home stores or gift stores.

▶ "Borrow your cake knife or toasting glasses from a friend or family member. This is one thing people get for their wedding that they probably won't use much, if ever again. They'll be honored to lend the set to you."

~ Deanna H., Detroit, MI

## BAKERY COMPARISON CHART

| Questions | POSSIBILITY 1 |
|---|---|
| What is the name of the bakery? | |
| What is the bakery's website and e-mail? | |
| What is the name and phone number of my contact person? | |
| How long have you been in business? | |
| What are your wedding cake specialties? | |
| What types of icings and fillings can I choose from? | |
| Do you offer free tasting of your wedding cakes? | |
| Are your wedding cakes fresh or frozen? | |
| How far in advance should I order my cake? | |
| Can you make a groom's cake? | |
| Do you lend, rent, or sell cake knives? | |
| What is the cost per serving of my desired cake? | |
| What is your cake pillar and plate rental fee? | |
| Is this fee refundable upon the return of these items? | |
| When must these items be returned? | |
| What is your cake delivery and setup fee? | |
| What is your payment/cancellation policy? | |

| POSSIBILITY 2 | POSSIBILITY 3 |
|---|---|
|  |  |
|  |  |
|  |  |
|  |  |
|  |  |
|  |  |
|  |  |
|  |  |
|  |  |
|  |  |
|  |  |
|  |  |
|  |  |
|  |  |
|  |  |
|  |  |

## CAKE TASTING CHART

### Bakery Option 1

Company Name: _____ Contact Person: _____

| Flavor | Price Per Slice | Notes |
|--------|-----------------|-------|
| 1) | $ | |
| 2) | $ | |
| 3) | $ | |

### Bakery Option 2

Company Name: _____ Contact Person: _____

| Flavor | Price Per Slice | Notes |
|--------|-----------------|-------|
| 1) | $ | |
| 2) | $ | |
| 3) | $ | |

### Bakery Option 3

Company Name: _____ Contact Person: _____

| Flavor | Price Per Slice | Notes |
|--------|-----------------|-------|
| 1) | $ | |
| 2) | $ | |
| 3) | $ | |

# Jessica & Tyler

## Total Spent: $7,325

**April 17, 2010 • Monterey, California • 35 guests**
**Photography by Max Wanger, www.maxwanger.com**
**Invitation photo by Jessica Quadra, www.jessicaquadra.com**

## Budget Breakdown

| | | | | |
|---|---|---|---|---|
| Attire | $1,275 | | Bar | $450 |
| Stationery | $200 | | Music | $500 |
| Ceremony Site | $0 | | Bakery | $150 |
| Photography | $3,000 | | Flowers | $300 |
| Videography | N/A | | Décor & Rental Items | $125 |
| Reception Site | $0 | | Miscellaneous | $125 |
| Food | $1,200 | | Total | $7,325 |

"Tyler proposed under a beautiful cypress tree on the Monterey Peninsula, almost exactly one year before our wedding date. We call it 'The Crooked Tree,'" says Jessica of her and Tyler's spring wedding. Her brother, an artist, incorporated the same tree in their custom invitations, and the couple weaved their Coastal Californian and Latin American influences throughout their intimate affair. "Having a small guest list of 35 people allowed us to keep the costs down," says the bride, who is actually a wedding photographer herself. "We wanted it to feel intimate and really us."

## FROM THE BRIDE
We're huge John Steinbeck fans, so we love visiting the Monterey Peninsula, where so many of his novels take place. I wanted some elements of our

backgrounds to come through — some Latin American influence and some Coastal Californian influence. The setting provided this alone, but our ring pillow was also made with a handkerchief of a map of California.

## STATIONERY
My brother, Carlos Quadra, whose work is inspired by Latin American

folkloric art, painted our invitation and map for us. He painted us under The Crooked Tree, and I had the cards printed. I used Photoshop to use parts of the painting for our RSVP cards. I designed our menu cards as well, with Mexican *papeles picados* (paper flags) across the top.

## ATTIRE

I fell in love with a Monique Lhuillier gown that cost more than my entire wedding budget, so I had a local designer in Orange County make my dress, inspired by the original. Her name is Dorie Kong of L'Mode Bridal. She did a fantastic job, and it cost me less than $1,000. My hairpiece was from ban.do. — I love their pieces! Tyler's suit was from J. Crew and his tie was from Zara.

## PHOTOGRAPHY

We did a "First Look" rather than waiting to see each other until the ceremony. Our photographer, Max Wanger, said Tyler's was the best groom's reaction he'd ever seen! I felt anxious up until the moment I saw Tyler. Seeing his reaction was so sweet and exciting, and when it came time for the ceremony, I was so present. Walking down the aisle toward him, I was 100 percent nerves-free.

## CEREMONY

Our dear friend, Amanda Stuart, officiated the ceremony and did an amazing job. She collected stories via email from our friends and families about us individually and as a couple and integrated these into our

ceremony. She told the story of our relationship and broke each section up into "chapters." At one moment, she had us pause and take a look at each person there and it was such an emotional feeling. We realized all the effort we put into planning the wedding and getting everyone together came through. The experience was my favorite part of the day.

If you're not having a religious ceremony or ceremony in a house of worship, I highly recommend asking a close friend or family member to officiate. It makes things more personal and meaningful. Shooting weddings, I've seen a lot of ceremonies, and it's always those weddings that are most memorable. The ceremony should be the most important part of the day — not your flowers, not your cake. Put time into planning your ceremony and don't be afraid to tell your officiant exactly what you want it to be. We also had a mariachi trio sing at the ceremony site.

## RECEPTION

Our reception was at Esteban's, a restaurant specializing in Spanish tapas, at Casa Munras Hotel in Monterey. We had originally booked the reception at a local restaurant only to learn that we had been double-booked just one month before the wedding! Casa Munras's event coordinator, Susan, came to the rescue. She was incredibly accommodating and had our spot and menu booked within a week. Phew!

We had wine with dinner and held the bar open for cocktail hour before dinner, but had a limit. The restaurant didn't charge a site fee; instead there was just a minimum per person. Spanish tapas was far less expensive than if we would have had a full dinner menu. We didn't hire a DJ, but made a playlist using my iPod.

## BAKERY
We had a croquembouche (French "wedding cake" comprised of a tower of cream puffs) made by Pâtisserie Bechler in Pacific Grove. I made our cake topper out of clay I bought at Michael's. It turned out better than I expected!

## FLOWERS
My friend works for an awesome wholesale flower company based in Carlsbad, California. He worked with me on choosing my flowers, mostly ranunculus, and had them shipped to Monterey the day before the wedding. My mom made all the centerpieces, boutonnieres, corsages and bouquets.

## ADVICE
I would definitely recommend that brides enlist talented friends or family members to help! Also, having a smaller guest list means you have many more options.

# Flowers

FLOWERS ADD BEAUTY, FRAGRANCE, AND COLOR
to your wedding. A breathtaking bouquet or
unique floral centerpiece gives your wedding
a special style and romance. You may also
want to use flowers or ribbons to mark the
aisle pews and add color.

## BRIDE'S BOUQUET

The bridal bouquet is one of the most important elements of the bride's attire and deserves special attention. Start by selecting the color and shape of the bouquet. The bridal bouquet should be carried low enough so that all the intricate details of your gown are visible.

**Options:** There are many colors, scents, sizes, shapes, and styles of bouquets to choose from. Popular styles are the cascade, cluster, posy, contemporary, waterfall, and hand-tied bouquets.

The traditional bridal bouquet is made of white flowers. Stephanotis, gardenias, white roses, orchids, and lilies of the valley are popular choices for an all-white bouquet.

If you prefer a colorful bouquet, you may want to consider using roses, tulips, stock, peonies, freesia, and gerbera, which come in a wide variety of colors.

Using scented flowers in your bouquet will evoke memories of your wedding day whenever you smell them in the future. Popular fragrant flowers are gardenias, freesia, stephanotis, bouvardia, and narcissus.

Some flowers carry centuries of

symbolism. Consider stephanotis —tradition regards it as the bridal good-luck flower! Pimpernel signifies change; white flowers radiate innocence; forget-me-nots indicate true love; and ivy stands for friendship, fidelity, and matrimony — the three essentials for a happy marriage.

No flower, however, has as much symbolism for brides as the orange blossom, having at least 700 years of nuptial history. Its unusual ability to simultaneously bear flowers and produce fruit symbolizes the fusion of beauty, personality, and fertility.

**Things to Consider:** Your flowers should complement the season, your gown, your color scheme, your attendants' attire, and the style and formality of your wedding. When you visit your florist, bring a photo or description of your dress and your wedding party's attire. You don't want an elaborate bouquet to overwhelm you; likewise, you don't want a small bouquet to get lost next to a ballgown. Typically, the bigger the dress, the bigger the bouquet.

Whatever flowers you select, final arrangements should be made well in advance of your wedding date to ensure availability. Confirm your final order and delivery time a few days before the wedding. Have the flowers delivered before the photographer arrives so that you can include them in your pre-ceremony photos.

In determining the size of your bouquet, consider your gown and your overall stature. Carry a smaller bouquet if you're petite or if your gown is fairly ornate. A long, cascading bouquet complements a fairly simple gown or a tall or larger bride. Arm bouquets look best when resting naturally in the crook of your arm. For a natural, fresh-picked look, have your florist put together a cluster of flowers tied together with a ribbon. For a Victorian appeal, carry a nosegay or a basket filled with flowers. Or carry a Bible or other family heirloom decorated with just a few flowers. For a contemporary look, you may want to consider carrying an arrangement of calla lilies or other long-stemmed flower over your arm. For a dramatic statement, carry a single stem of your favorite flower!

If your bouquet includes delicate flowers that will not withstand hours of heat or a lack of water, make sure your florist uses a bouquet holder to keep them fresh. If you want to carry fresh-cut stems without a bouquet holder, make sure the flowers you select are hardy enough to go without water for the duration of your ceremony and reception.

Price Range: $25 - $400

▶ Avoid exotic or out-of-season flowers that will need to be shipped in from a distant location — the cost will be significantly higher. For instance, peonies, a big, beautiful flower that is very popular for weddings, will cost about $4 a stem in the spring, but about $15 in the fall, the flower's off-season. Select flowers that are in bloom and plentiful in your area at the time of your wedding.

▶ Be aware of which flowers are inexpensive and which may be out of your budget. For example, daisies, sunflowers, carnations, camellias, gladiolus, hydrangea, chrysanthemums, Oriental lilies and Dendrobium orchids are all reasonably priced. Roses, ranunculus, tulips and freesia vary in cost based on the season and availability. Expensive blooms that brides on a budget may want to avoid include calla lilies, lilies of the valley, delphiniums, Hawaiian orchids, and Stargazer and Casablanca lilies. In addition, all-white bouquets, with flowers such as stephanotis and gardenias, are typically expensive, because white flowers are delicate and tend to bruise easily.

▶ Allow your florist to emphasize your colors using more reasonable, seasonal flowers to achieve your overall look. If you have a favorite flower that is costly or out of season, consider using silk for that one flower.

▶ Use a few stems of a larger flower, such as hydrangeas, peonies, or gerbera, rather than buying more stems of a smaller flower.

▶ Pad your bouquet to make it look more full, using baby's breath, ivy, eucalyptus, succulents and more. A good florist will know tricks for making a few flowers go a long way.

▶ Avoid labor-intensive designs, such as cascade and waterfall bouquets. Also, flowers that require wiring or floral taping, such as orchids, sweet peas, and other delicate flowers, will cost more than thick, long-stemmed flowers like gerbera, roses and carnations.

- ▶ Give your florist the OK to substitute a similar flower in the event that prices for your first choice go up. Floral prices fluctuate all the time. The roses you chose, in the color you chose, may be a different price 6 months before your wedding than two weeks before the wedding. Ask your florist to make a judgment call, but to run it by you. For instance, ranunculus can make a beautiful alternative to roses in a pinch.

- ▶ Avoid scheduling your wedding near holidays, such as Valentine's Day, Easter and Mother's Day, when the price of flowers is higher. Purchasing flowers just after these holidays, however, can mean a discount. For instance, roses are deeply discounted after Valentine's Day.

- ▶ Purchase flowers from a wholesale market, farmer's market, online or even the grocery store, and trim, tie and arrange the bouquets yourself. You should ask your bridal party or other friends and family to help with this project. Also, be aware that flowers will need to be stored in a cool place to avoid wilting. Tutorials for tying bouquets (and creating centerpieces and boutonnieres, too) can be found online. Try YouTube.com for plenty of DIY bouquet videos.

- ▶ Skip the bouquet toss (a tradition some couples find antiquated anyway) to avoid paying for a second tossing bouquet.

## Real Couples' Weddings

- ▶ "I heard a bride say the one thing she would do over about her wedding was to get married in peony season. To me, this means she either spent way too much money on shipping in an out-of-season flower, or she settled for budget-friendly flowers that weren't what she truly wanted. The lesson here is be flexible — either don't get your heart set on one flower or else make room in your budget for your top priority."
  ~ Kathy B., Charleston, SC

- ▶ "I liked the delicate look of Lily of the Valley, but they are one of the most expensive flowers, come to find out. Instead, I went with a bouquet of baby's breath tied with a pale blue ribbon. It looked like lace; I loved it. The best part was I got 10 bunches of baby's breath for the price of 1 bunch of Lily of the Valley!"
  ~ Courtney B., Fort Wayne, IN

## MAID OF HONOR & BRIDESMAIDS' BOUQUETS

Choose a bouquet style for your attendants that complements the formality of your wedding and their dresses. The maid of honor's bouquet can be somewhat larger or of a different color than the rest of the bridesmaids' bouquets. This will help to set her apart from the others. The bridesmaids' bouquets should complement the bridal bouquet, but are generally smaller in size.

Options: Bridesmaids' bouquets can be identical or can each be a different flower that make up the bridal bouquet.

Things to Consider: If your bridesmaids will be wearing floral print dresses, select flowers that subtly complement the floral print.

Price Range:  $25 - $100

### Ideas to Save Money

▶ Because every attendant will carry flowers, consider keeping the size of your wedding party down to accommodate your floral budget.

▶ Using a single type of flower for all the bridesmaids' bouquets can save money. You can buy them wholesale in bulk.

▶ Ask for a posy bouquet, a smaller version of a nosegay, which is a tight cluster of flowers. Then have your attendants decorate the cake table or other area of the reception with their bouquets.

▶ Have your attendants carry a single stemmed rose, lily, or other long-stemmed flower for an elegant look that also saves money.

### Real Couples' Weddings

▶ "I wanted the full, open look of peonies and roses for my March wedding, but the price was going to be prohibitive. My florist suggested ranunculus in bright colors, mixed with sunflowers, which was a different style than I'd planned, but I fell in love with the bouquets."
~ Vanessa T., Graham, NC

# MAID OF HONOR & BRIDESMAIDS' HAIRPIECES

You may want your maid of honor and bridesmaids to wear flowers in their hair, especially for an outdoor or garden wedding.

**Things to Consider:** If you use real flowers in the hairpiece, they must be hardy and able to withstand the heat.

**Price Range:** $8 - $100

## Ideas to Save Money

▶ Consider using artificial flowers for the hairpieces as long as they are in keeping with the flowers carried in bouquets. A simple DIY project can be to purchase silk flowers from a crafts store, remove the stems, and hot glue the bloom to a hair clip or headband.

## Real Couples' Weddings

▶ "I originally wanted my bridesmaids to wear large white flowers in their hair, but the cost of the stems seemed silly, plus it would have taken the hairstylist an extra hour to wire in the flowers. Instead, I found beautiful flower headbands at a Forever 21 store for $3 each. In the end, there was no difference between a real flower and a silk flower, and the girls look great in my photos."
~ Stephanie L., Tacoma, WA

## FLOWER GIRL'S HAIRPIECE

Flower girls often wear a wreath of flowers as a hairpiece.

**Options:** This is another place where artificial flowers may be used, but they must be in keeping with the flowers carried by members of the bridal party.

**Things to Consider:** Be sure to give your florist your flower girl's head measurements so the wreath is the correct size. If the flowers used for the hairpiece are not a sturdy and long-lived variety, a ribbon, bow, or hat might be a safer choice.

**Price Range:** $8 - $75

## BRIDE'S GOING AWAY CORSAGE

Traditionally, couples would leave right from their weddings to go on their honeymoons; thus, they changed into a going away outfit, complete with floral corsage. If you choose to do this, have your florist create a corsage that echoes the beauty of your bouquet.

**Things to Consider:** Put a protective shield under lilies when using them as a corsage, as their anthers will stain fabric.

**Price Range:** $10 - $50

### Ideas to Save Money

▶ Ask your florist if he or she can design your bridal bouquet in such a way that the center flowers may be removed and worn as a corsage. Or omit this corsage altogether.

## FAMILY MEMBERS' CORSAGES

The groom is responsible for providing flowers for his mother, the bride's mother, and the grandmothers. The officiant, if female, may also be given a corsage to reflect her important role in the ceremony. The corsages don't have to be identical, but they should be coordinated with the color of their dresses.

**Options:** The groom may order flowers that can be pinned to a lapel or worn around a wrist. He should ask which style the women prefer, and if a particular color is needed to coordinate with their dresses. Gardenias, camellias, white orchids, or cymbidium orchids are excellent choices for corsages, as they go well with any outfit.

**Things to Consider:** The groom may also want to consider ordering corsages for other close family members, such as sisters and aunts. This will add a little to your floral expenses but will make these female family members feel more included in your wedding and will let guests know that they are related to the bride and groom. Many women do not like to wear corsages, so the groom should check with the people involved before ordering the flowers.

**Price Range:** $10 - $35

▶ Ask your florist to recommend reasonable flowers for corsages. For instance, dendrobium orchids are well-priced and make lovely corsages.

▶ "Corsages often get in the way and not all women like to wear them. Instead, give each important woman a single stem of a beautiful flower as a gift and thank you. A single stem will cost much less than a corsage, which requires labor."
~ Kate M., Las Vegas, NV

## GROOM'S BOUTONNIERE

The groom wears his boutonniere on the left lapel, nearest to his heart.

**Options:** Boutonnieres are generally a single blossom, such as a rosebud, calla lily, freesia, or a miniature carnation. If a single bud is used for the wedding party, have the groom wear two buds, or add a sprig of greenery to differentiate him from the groomsmen.

**Things to Consider:** Be careful when using alstroemeria as a boutonniere, as its sap can be harmful if it enters the bloodstream.

**Price Range:** $4 - $25

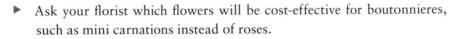

▶ Ask your florist which flowers will be cost-effective for boutonnieres, such as mini carnations instead of roses.

▶ Make your own boutonnieres out of non-floral materials to save money. Work with feathers, shells, felt, buttons and more. Or, work with a theme, such as fishing, golf, etc.

▶ "My husband and his groomsmen went golfing for his bachelor party, so, instead of floral boutonnieres, I tied a cluster of colored wooden golf tees together with twine and glued them to a flat safety pin. Simple and cute!"

~ Rebecca S., Columbia, SC

## USHERS/OTHER FAMILY MEMBERS' BOUTONNIERES

The groom gives each man in his wedding party a boutonniere to wear on his left lapel. The officiant, if male, may also be given a boutonniere to reflect his important role in the ceremony. The ring bearer may or may not wear a boutonniere.

Options: Boutonnieres are generally a single blossom, such as a rosebud, calla lily, freesia, or a miniature carnation.

Things to Consider: The groom should also consider ordering boutonnieres for other close family members such as fathers, grandfathers, and brothers. This will add a little to your floral expenses, but will make these male family members feel more included in your wedding and will let guests know that they are related to the bride and groom.

Price Range: $3 - $15

Ideas to Save Money 💡

▶ Ask your florist which flowers will be cost-effective.

▶ Make your own boutonnieres out of non-floral materials, such as feathers, shells, felt, buttons, golf tees, and more.

Real Couples' Weddings ❝❞

▶ "We used fake flowers for our boutonnieres, although I'm sure no one could tell. The only trick is to combine real greenery if you want ivy or ferns or large leaves, because silk flowers look real but plastic greenery does not."

~ Morgan V., Cincinnati, OH

## MAIN ALTAR

The purpose of flowers at the main altar is to direct the guests' visual attention toward the front of the church or synagogue and to the bridal couple. Your officiant's advice, or that of the altar guild or florist, can be most helpful in choosing flowers for the altar.

**Options:** If your ceremony is outside, decorate the arch, gazebo, or other structure serving as the altar with flowers or greenery. In a Jewish ceremony, vows are said under a Chuppah, which is placed at the altar and covered with greens and fresh flowers.

**Things to Consider:** In choosing floral accents, consider the décor of your ceremony site. Some churches and synagogues are ornate enough and don't need extra flowers. Too many arrangements would get lost in the architectural splendor. Select a few dramatic showpieces that will complement the existing décor. Be sure to ask if there are any restrictions on flowers at the church or synagogue. Remember, decorations should be determined by the size and style of the building, the formality of the wedding, the preferences of the bride, the cost, and the regulations of the particular site.

**Price Range:** $50 - $3,000

### Ideas to Save Money

▶ Choose a ceremony site that is already beautiful. For instance, many outdoor venues won't need flowers, or a church with candlelight and stained glass windows may not need extra decorations.

▶ Your ceremony site may have decorations you can use free of charge, especially things like poinsettias and candles around the holidays. Be sure to ask.

▶ Reuse the main altar floral decorations at your reception site. Just consider the cost of transportation and setup at both locations.

### Real Couples' Weddings

▶ "Instead of flowers at the altar we used candelabras. They were inexpensive antique pieces and gave the area a romantic glow."
~ Laura A., Austin, TX

## AISLE PEWS

Flowers, candles, or ribbons are often used to mark the aisle pews and add color.

**Options:** A cluster of flowers, a cascade of greens, or a cascade of flowers and ribbons are all popular choices.

**Things to Consider:** Use hardy flowers that can tolerate being handled as pew ornaments. Gardenias and camellias, for example, are too sensitive. Avoid using allium in your aisle decorations as they have an odor of onions.

**Price Range:** $5 - $75

### Ideas to Save Money

▶ It is not necessary to decorate all of the aisle pews, or any at all. To save money, decorate only the reserved family pews. Or decorate every second or third pew.

▶ Consider a non-floral element to save money. Mason jars with tea lights or large seashells hung from ribbons can be lovely along the aisle.

### Real Couples' Weddings

▶ "We tied sand dollars and starfish that we bought for $1 or less apiece on the chairs in the aisle. We moved them onto tables after the ceremony."
~ Jess P., Naples, FL

## RECEPTION SITE

Flowers add beauty, fragrance, and color to your reception. Flowers for the reception, like everything else, should fit your overall style and color scheme. Flowers can help transform a stark reception hall into a warm, inviting, and colorful room.

**Things to Consider:** You can rent indoor plants or small trees to give your indoor reception a garden-like atmosphere.

Price Range: $300 - $3,000

▶ You can save money by taking flowers from the ceremony to the reception site for decorations. However, you must coordinate this move carefully to avoid having your guests arrive at an undecorated reception room.

▶ Use greenery rather than flowers to fill large areas. Trees and garlands of ivy can give a dramatic impact for little money. Decorate them with strands of inexpensive lights.

▶ Have your reception outside in a beautiful garden or by the water, surrounded by nature's own beauty, and use only small table decorations.

▶ "We were having our ceremony and reception in a banquet room, so I needed to transform a completely blank space into the wedding of my dreams. I wanted trees with twinkling lights to line the aisle, but it would have cost $20,000 to have live trees brought in! Instead, we hand-made them using birch tree branches we cut down ourselves. We planted them in large containers I got from a local nursery. We bought white silk flowers in three sizes from a crafts store and hand-glued them into the branches, along with mini pearls and crystals strung from fishing line that hung from the branches. We added inexpensive lights, and they looked absolutely gorgeous! We spent $1,000 on materials and they made our entire venue glow."
~ Jenny G., Manhattan, NY

## HEAD TABLE

The head table is where the wedding party will sit during the reception. This important table should be decorated with a larger or more dramatic centerpiece than the guest tables.

Price Range: $100 - $600

▶ Use a small, short centerpiece, which is much less expensive than a tall one. Consider a tightly packed cluster of carnation blooms. A good florist knows how to make even inexpensive flowers look elegant and beautiful.

▶ Decorate the head table with the bridal and attendants' bouquets.

## TABLE CENTERPIECES

At a reception where guests are seated, a small flower arrangement may be placed on each table.

Options: Candles, mirrors, water centerpieces and flowers are popular choices for table centerpieces. However, the options are endless. Just be creative! An arrangement of shells, for example, makes a very nice centerpiece for a seaside reception. Floating candles in a low, round bowl make a romantic centerpiece for an evening reception.

Things to Consider: The arrangements should complement the table linens and the size of the table, and should be kept low enough so as not to hinder conversation among guests seated across from each other. Consider using a centerpiece that your guests can take home as a memento of your wedding.

Avoid using highly fragrant flowers, like narcissus, on tables where food is being served or eaten.

Price Range: $100 - $1,000

▶ Use a few large, beautiful blooms instead of numerous small flowers.

▶ Instead of flowers, use inexpensive themed decorations as centerpieces. Consider paper lanterns and take-out boxes to create Asian-inspired style. Or, consider decorations that represent you as a couple; for instance, a pair of writers might decorate with vintage books.

- Shop at antique stores and on eBay for vintage pieces like mason jars, milk crates, vases, and glass bowls, which can be filled with flowers, stones, or buttons for inexpensive, pretty centerpieces.

- Mix non-floral natural elements with flowers to cut back on your flower order. Stones, fruit, shells, and succulents make for a unique, modern look when mixed with a few flowers.

- Candles give the room a warm, romantic glow and can be bought cheaply, in bulk. Group vases, bowls or mason jars filled with candles of different heights and sizes, with or without flowers to complement them.

- Use groups of small potted flowering plants or succulents as center-pieces. After the reception, you can give them as gifts.

**Real Couples' Weddings**

- "We filled square and rectangular vases with oranges, lemons and limes for our spring wedding. We went to a Mexican market the day before the wedding and got everything very cheap — like limes for 19 cents!"
  ~ Liz M., Tucson, AZ

## BUFFET TABLE

If buffet tables are used, have some type of floral arrangement on the tables to add color and beauty to your display of food.

**Things to Consider:** Avoid placing certain flowers, such as carnations, snapdragons, or the star of Bethlehem, next to buffet displays of fruits or vegetables, as they are extremely sensitive to the gasses emitted by these foods and may wilt.

**Price Range:** $50 - $300

**Ideas to Save Money**

- Instead of flowers, opt for whole fruits and bunches of berries. Figs add a festive touch. Pineapples are a sign of hospitality. Vegetables offer an endless array of options to decorate with.

▶ Decorate the buffet table with fragrant herbs used in the food you are serving, such as basil, rosemary, mint and more.

## CAKE TABLE

The wedding cake is often one of the focal points at the reception. Decorate the cake table with flowers.

Price Range: $30 - $300

### Ideas to Save Money

▶ Have your bridesmaids place their bouquets on the cake table during the reception.

▶ Decorate the cake top only and surround the base of the cake with greenery and a few loose flowers.

### Real Couples' Weddings

▶ "Instead of ordering a lot of flowers for our cake table, we decorated it with just a few roses and framed photos from our engagement shoot and my bridal shoot. Guests stopped to really admire the photos and the cake."
~ Alison W., Tiburon, CA

## CAKE

Flowers are a beautiful addition to a wedding cake and are commonly seen as a cake topper or spilling out between the cake tiers.

Things to Consider: Use only nonpoisonous flowers, and have your florist — not the caterer — design the floral decorations for your cake. A florist will be able to blend the cake decorations into your overall floral theme.

Price Range: $20 - $100

► Have your baker design realistic-looking flowers out of fondant or sugar paste instead of using real flowers.

## FLORAL DELIVERY/SETUP

Most florists charge a fee to deliver flowers to the ceremony and reception sites and to arrange them onsite.

**Things to Consider:** Make sure your florist knows where your sites are and what time to arrive for setup.

**Price Range:** $25 - $200

► If you're having a small wedding or a wedding with very few floral decorations, purchase your own flowers wholesale and ask family and friends to help you set them up.

## Bride's Bouquet

Color Scheme: _____

Style: _____

Flowers: _____

_____

Greenery: _____

Other (Ribbons, etc.): _____


## Maid of Honor's Bouquet

Color Scheme: _____

Style: _____

Flowers: _____

_____

Greenery: _____

Other (Ribbons, etc.): _____


## Bridesmaids' Bouquets

Color Scheme: _____

Style: _____

Flowers: _____

_____

Greenery: _____

Other (Ribbons, etc.): _____

## BOUQUETS AND FLOWERS

### Flower Girl's Bouquet

Color Scheme: _____

Style: _____

Flowers: _____

_____

Greenery: _____

Other (Ribbons, etc.): _____


### Other

Groom's Boutonniere: _____

_____

Ushers' Boutonnieres: _____

_____

Other Family Members' Boutonnieres: _____

_____

Mother of the Bride Corsage: _____

_____

Mother of the Groom Corsage: _____

_____

Altar or Chuppah: _____

_____

Steps to Altar or Chuppah: _____

_____

## Other (Cont.)

Pews: _____

_____

Entrance to the Ceremony: _____

_____

Entrance to the Reception: _____

_____

Receiving Line: _____

_____

Head Table: _____

_____

Parents' Table: _____

_____

Guest Table: _____

_____

Cake Table: _____

_____

Serving Table (Buffet, Dessert): _____

_____

Gift Table: _____

_____

Other: _____

_____

## FLORIST COMPARISON CHART

| Questions | POSSIBILITY 1 |
|---|---|
| What is the name of the florist? | |
| What is the website and e-mail of the florist? | |
| What is the address of the florist? | |
| What are your business hours? | |
| What is the name and phone number of my contact person? | |
| How many years of professional floral experience do you have? | |
| What percentage of your business is dedicated to weddings? | |
| Do you have access to out-of-season flowers? | |
| Will you visit my wedding sites to make floral recommendations? | |
| Can you preserve my bridal bouquet? | |
| Do you rent vases and candleholders? | |
| Can you provide silk flowers? | |
| What is the cost of the desired bridal bouquet? | |
| What is the cost of the desired boutonniere/corsage? | |
| Do you have liability insurance? | |
| What are your delivery/setup fees? | |
| What is your payment/cancellation policy? | |

| POSSIBILITY 2 | POSSIBILITY 3 |
| --- | --- |
|  |  |
|  |  |
|  |  |
|  |  |
|  |  |
|  |  |
|  |  |
|  |  |
|  |  |
|  |  |
|  |  |
|  |  |
|  |  |
|  |  |
|  |  |
|  |  |

## FLOWERS AND THEIR SEASONS

| FLOWER | Winter | Spring | Summer | Fall |
|---|---|---|---|---|
| Allium | | X | X | |
| Alstroemeria | X | X | X | X |
| Amaryllis | X | | X | |
| Anemone | X | X | | X |
| Aster | X | X | X | X |
| Baby's Breath | X | X | X | X |
| Bachelor's Button | X | X | X | X |
| Billy Buttons | | X | X | |
| Bird of Paradise | X | X | X | X |
| Bouvardia | X | X | X | X |
| Calla Lily | X | X | X | X |
| Carnation | X | X | X | X |
| Celosia | | X | X | |
| Chrysanthemum | X | X | X | X |
| Daffodils | | X | | |
| Dahlia | | | X | X |
| Delphinium | | | X | X |
| Eucalyptus | X | X | X | X |
| Freesia | X | X | X | X |
| Gardenia | X | X | X | X |
| Gerbera | X | X | X | X |
| Gladiolus | X | X | X | X |
| Iris | X | X | X | X |
| Liatris | X | X | X | X |
| Lily | X | X | X | X |

| FLOWER | Winter | Spring | Summer | Fall |
|---|---|---|---|---|
| Lily of the Valley | | X | | |
| Lisianthus | | X | X | X |
| Narcissus | X | X | | X |
| Nerine | X | X | X | X |
| Orchid (Cattleya) | X | X | X | X |
| Orchid (Cymbidium) | X | X | X | X |
| Peony | | X | | |
| Pincushion | | | X | |
| Protea | X | | | X |
| Queen Anne's Lace | | | X | |
| Ranunculas | | X | | |
| Rose | X | X | X | X |
| Saponaria | | | X | |
| Snapdragon | | X | X | X |
| Speedwell | | | X | |
| Star of Bethlehem | X | | | X |
| Statice | X | X | X | X |
| Stephanotis | X | X | X | X |
| Stock | X | X | X | X |
| Sunflower | | X | X | X |
| Sweet Pea | | X | | |
| Tuberose | | | X | X |
| Tulip | X | X | | |
| Waxflower | X | X | | |

# WEDDING PLANNING NOTES

# Jennifer & Brian

Total Spent: $5,000

**March 31, 2007 • Captiva Island, Florida • 30 guests**
**Photography by Jerri Lynn, www.photographybyjerrilynn.com**

## Budget Breakdown

| | | | | |
|---|---|---|---|---|
| Attire | $1,100 | Bar | $200 |
| Stationery | $50 | Music | $0 |
| Ceremony Site | $300 | Bakery | $50 |
| Photography | $300 | Flowers | $200 |
| Videography | N/A | Décor & Rental Items | $0 |
| Reception Site | $0 | Miscellaneous | $800 |
| Food | $2,000 | **Total** | **$5,000** |

Jennifer and Brian had a vision for their Florida wedding: a romantic ceremony on the beach, followed by a casual night of dinner, music and laughter with an intimate group of loved ones. The couple chose details that were sweet and simple and in keeping with their relaxed, beachy theme, including starfish blended with the flowers and leather flip-flops for the men and ring bearers. Not only did Jennifer and Brian create their perfect beachside wedding day, but they actually went under their original estimate, leaving room in their budget for a luxurious wedding night cottage overlooking the waves.

## FROM THE BRIDE

My husband and I had a fabulous beach wedding in Captiva Island, Florida — on a budget! We wanted to be with our closest friends and family, and for everyone who came to enjoy the natural beauty of the area. We kept a lot of wedding details simple but, the day of the wedding, we splurged on spa appointments for myself and my bridesmaid and on a fishing excursion for my husband and his best man. Our original budget was $7,500, and we actually came in at $5,000. We used the extra $2,500 to splurge on a wedding night cottage. Because we didn't take our honeymoon for a few months after the wedding, we spent our wedding night on Captiva Island and then spent time with our families for the next few days.

## ATTIRE & BEAUTY

For my dress, I chose an elegant sleeveless evening gown. I spent about $500 on my dress, shoes and veil. I spent another $200 for the dress for my sister, who was my bridesmaid, and my niece, who was the flower girl. We also spent about $500 for casual tuxedos. The guys wore flip-flops, which avoided renting shoes. For $100, my hairdresser came out to our location.

## CEREMONY

We chose to get married at Chapel by the Sea. We had our wedding on the beach at sunset and took photos by the ocean and in the chapel. We saved money on flowers and decorations because the beach was so naturally beautiful. We were joined by an intimate group of family and friends, and as I walked down the sandy aisle to meet my groom, I was surrounded by the 30 people dearest to me.

## RECEPTION

After the ceremony, our guests walked down the beach to a restaurant just off the sand called Keylime Bistro. It was a beautiful evening, and as we walked, people were cheering, and everyone was standing as we entered the patio of the restaurant.

## FOOD & BAKERY

Since we planned our wedding in the height of the season, it would have been very expensive to rent the whole restaurant or entire patio. So, we worked with the restaurant to give us one long table for our group of 30. We arranged for a special menu where our guests could choose from five different items. The $2,000 we spent on dinner was much less than if we would have rented a formal reception hall. I also worked with a local baker to make a small cake covered with chocolate seashells.

## FLOWERS

A local florist and I worked together to keep the bouquets very simple, with beautiful roses and carnations in tropical colors. I brought her a variety of shells and starfish to incorporate with the flowers, which filled out the florals for very little money.

## MUSIC

The entertainment was already included in our venue since Keylime Bistro has a live entertainer on the patio. One couple at another table even bought us his CD in exchange for a piece of our cake!

## GIFTS

Instead of purchasing expensive bride and groom's gifts, we made sentimental gifts for each other. We wrote letters, and I gave my husband a book of keepsakes that I had kept since we met, including emails and letters to each other.

## ADVICE

We had such a great time at our wedding! It was so romantic and personal.

I'd recommend that brides with a smaller budget concentrate on what is most significant to them. For us, it was spending quality time with the most important people in our life.

And don't think you have to hire an expensive professional for everything. We made our own invitations with photos that we had our friend take. We used another friend to do the wedding photography and then printed the photos and put them into an album ourselves.

# Transportation

WEDDING-DAY TRANSPORTATION CAN be as fancy or as simple as fits your personality, venue and budget. From a horse-drawn carriage or stretch limousine to a borrowed vintage car or bicycle built for two, couples can arrive in style in any way they choose.

## TRANSPORTATION

Normally, a procession to the ceremony begins with the bride's mother and several of the bride's attendants in the first vehicle. If desired, you can provide a second vehicle for the rest of the attendants. The bride and her father will go in the last vehicle. This vehicle will also be used to transport the bride and groom to the reception site after the ceremony.

Options: There are various options for transportation. The most popular choice is a limousine, since it is large and open and can accommodate many people, as well as your bridal gown. If you would like to ride with your entire wedding party, consider riding in style in a trendy stretch-Hummer limo.

You can also choose to rent a car that symbolizes your personality as a couple. You might rent a luxury car, such as a Mercedes or Ferrari, or a vintage vehicle, such as a 1950s Thunderbird or 1930s Cadillac.

Things to Consider: Always make sure the transportation company you choose is fully licensed and has liability insurance. Do not pay the full amount until after the event.

Get everything in writing before

your wedding, including exact pickup times, requests for items like champagne glasses and ice, and the license plate number of the exact vehicle you want for your Big Day. Some companies will sell you with one vehicle and attempt to substitute a different vehicle on the actual day.

Don't forget to factor in the driver's gratuity when you price out transportation options. Drivers typically get a mandatory 15 to 20 percent tip, in addition to the hourly rental rate.

**Price Range:** $35 - $200 per hour

## Ideas to Save Money

▶ Consider hiring only one large limousine to transport you, your parents, and your attendants to the ceremony, and then you and your new husband from the ceremony to the reception.

▶ If you're not traveling far to the ceremony and reception venues, it may not make sense to pay for transportation, especially since limousines are typically booked on a three-hour-minimum basis.

▶ Rent a luxury or antique car for about $125 a day (as opposed to that much an hour). Ask a friend or family member to act as the driver.

▶ Rent a tandem or two-person bike to ride up to the reception on. This makes for fun photos and your guests will love the sight. You should be able to find tandem bike rentals for $30 or less a day.

▶ See if you have a family member or friend with an interesting car who wouldn't mind lending it to you for the wedding day.

▶ "We really wanted to rent a cool car to take us to the reception and for pictures, but we were having a hard time finding something in our budget that went with a Latin theme. This sounds crazy, but a week before the wedding, I actually approached a guy with an amazing low-rider convertible in a parking lot and asked if we could rent his car for an hour at the wedding. I threw out a figure and he accepted. I think he was really flattered that I liked his car so much, and I'm glad it worked out because the photos are great. Don't be afraid to think outside the box!"
~David D., Albuquerque, NM

# TRANSPORTATION COMPARISON CHART

| Questions | POSSIBILITY 1 |
|---|---|
| What is the name of the transportation service? | |
| What is the website and e-mail of the transportation service? | |
| What is the name and phone number of my contact person? | |
| How many years have you been in business? | |
| How many vehicles and drivers do you have available? | |
| What types of vehicles are available? | |
| Can you provide a back-up vehicle in case of an emergency or breakdown? | |
| What are the various sizes of vehicles available? | |
| How old are the vehicles? | |
| How do your drivers dress for weddings? | |
| What is the cost per hour? Two hours? Three hours? | |
| What is the minimum amount of time required to rent a vehicle? | |
| What is the price per hour of overtime? | |
| Do you provide or allow champagne or other alcohol in your vehicles? | |
| Do you have liability insurance? | |
| How much gratuity is expected? | |
| What is your payment/cancellation policy? | |

| POSSIBILITY 2 | POSSIBILITY 3 |
|---|---|
|  |  |
|  |  |
|  |  |
|  |  |
|  |  |
|  |  |
|  |  |
|  |  |
|  |  |
|  |  |
|  |  |
|  |  |
|  |  |
|  |  |
|  |  |
|  |  |
|  |  |

## WEDDING DAY TRANSPORTATION

### TO CEREMONY SITE

| Passenger | Pickup Time | Pickup Location | Vehicle/Driver |
|---|---|---|---|
| Bride | | | |
| Groom | | | |
| Bride's Parents | | | |
| Groom's Parents | | | |
| Bridesmaids | | | |
| Ushers | | | |
| Other: | | | |
| Other: | | | |
| Other: | | | |

### TO RECEPTION SITE

| Passenger | Pickup Time | Pickup Location | Vehicle/Driver |
|---|---|---|---|
| Bride and Groom | | | |
| Bride's Parents | | | |
| Groom's Parents | | | |
| Bridesmaids | | | |
| Ushers | | | |
| Other: | | | |
| Other: | | | |

# Rental Items

RENTALS ALLOW YOU TO HOST A RECEPTION in your own home or in less traditional locations, such as an art museum, a local park, or at the beach. Be sure to take into account the cost for all these rental items when creating your budget.

## CEREMONY ACCESSORIES

Ceremony rental accessories are the additional items needed for the ceremony but not included in the ceremony site fee.

Ceremony rental accessories may include the following items:

Aisle Runner:  A thin rug made of plastic, paper or cloth extending the length of the aisle. It is rolled out after the mothers are seated, just prior to the processional.  Plastic or paper doesn't work well on grass; but if you must use one of these types of runners, make sure the grass is clipped short.

Kneeling Cushion: A small cushion or pillow placed in front of the altar where the bride and groom kneel for their wedding blessing.

Arch (Christian): A white lattice or brass arch where the bride and groom exchange their vows, often decorated with flowers and greenery.

Chuppah (Jewish): A canopy under which a Jewish ceremony is performed, symbolizing cohabitation and consummation.

You may also need to consider renting audio equipment, aisle stanchions, candelabra, candles, candlelighters, chairs, heaters, a gift table, a guest book stand, and a canopy.

**Things to Consider:** Make sure the rental supplier has been in business for a good amount of time and has a good reputation. Reserve the items you need well in advance. Find out the company's payment, reservation, and cancellation policies.

Some companies allow you to reserve emergency items, such as heaters or canopies, without having to pay for them unless needed, in which case you would need to call the rental company a day or two in advance to request the items. If someone else requests the items you have reserved, the company should give you the right of first refusal.

**Price Range:** $100 - $500

## Ideas to Save Money

▶ Negotiate a package deal, if possible, by renting items for both the ceremony and the reception from the same supplier. Or consider renting these items from your florist so you only have to pay one delivery fee.

▶ Shop early and compare prices with several party rental suppliers, especially if you're marrying on a Saturday during a popular wedding month.

▶ Attempt to negotiate free delivery and setup with party rental suppliers in exchange for giving them your business.

## TENT/CANOPY

A large tent or canopy may be required for receptions held outdoors to protect you and your guests from the sun or rain. Tents and canopies can be expensive due to the labor involved in delivery and setup.

**Options:** Tents and canopies come in different sizes and shapes and with different amenities. Some have side flaps, heaters and cooling, and flooring for a lawn reception. Contact several party rental suppliers to discuss the options.

Things to Consider: Consider this cost when making a decision between an outdoor and an indoor reception. Be aware of whether you will need heating or cooling inside the tent, as well.

Price Range: $300 - $5,000

▶ If there is another couple hosting a wedding at your same venue during the same weekend, contact them about splitting the cost of a tent.

▶ Find a reception venue that has a tent onsite as an added feature to their wedding packages. That way, it can be set up quickly if the weather looks shaky on the morning of your wedding, and the venue can easily add the cost onto your bill.

▶ "We were married in early June in San Diego, which — despite what people think about Southern California — can mean gray skies and rain during that time of year. Our venue was a historic home that didn't allow for inside receptions, so we were worried about being rained out. We couldn't afford to rent the $2,000 tent on our budget, but we emailed the couple who was getting married at the same place the night before us and asked if they'd like to split the cost. We were glad they did when it started pouring during our cocktail hour!"
~ Kara D., San Diego, CA

## DANCE FLOOR

A dance floor will be provided by most hotels and clubs. However, if your reception site does not have a dance floor, you may need to rent one through your caterer or a party rental supplier.

Things to Consider: When comparing prices of dance floors, include the delivery and setup fees.

Price Range: $100 - $600

▶ "I looked into renting a dance floor for my daughter's wedding, and it was going to cost about $700. When I found one for purchase on Craigslist for $1,000, I decided to buy the dance floor in hopes of using it once and renting it out after the wedding. I already have one wedding booked, so I may actually be making money in the long run!"
~ Mary C., Atlanta, GA

## TABLES/CHAIRS

You will have to provide tables and chairs for your guests if your reception site or caterer doesn't provide them as part of their package. For a full meal, you will have to provide tables and seating for all guests. For a cocktail reception, you only need to provide tables and chairs for approximately 30 to 50 percent of your guests. Ask your caterer or reception site manager for advice.

Options: There are various types of tables and chairs to choose from. The most commonly used chairs for wedding receptions are white wooden or plastic chairs. The most common tables for receptions are round tables that seat eight guests. The most common head table arrangement is several rectangular tables placed end-to-end to seat your entire wedding party on one side, facing your guests. Contact various party rental suppliers to find out what types of chairs and tables they carry, as well as their price ranges.

Things to Consider: When comparing prices of renting tables and chairs, include the cost of delivery and setup.

Price Range: $3 - $10 per person

**Ideas to Save Money**

▶ Rent one set of chairs for the ceremony and ask guests to help you move them to the reception area, if the ceremony and reception are being held in the same location.

## LINENS/TABLEWARE

You will also need to provide linens and tableware for your reception if your reception site or caterer does not provide them as part of their package.

**Options:** For a sit-down reception where the meal is served by waiters and waitresses, tables are usually set with a cloth (usually white, but may be color-coordinated with the wedding), a centerpiece, and complete place settings. At a less formal buffet reception where guests serve themselves, tables are covered with a cloth, but place settings are not mandatory. The necessary plates and silverware may be located at the buffet table, next to the food.

**Things to Consider:** Linens and tableware depend on the formality of your reception. When comparing prices of linens and tableware, include the cost of delivery and setup.

**Price Range:** $3 - $25 per person

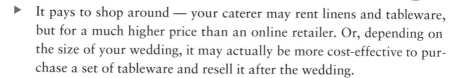

### Ideas to Save Money

▶  It pays to shop around — your caterer may rent linens and tableware, but for a much higher price than an online retailer. Or, depending on the size of your wedding, it may actually be more cost-effective to purchase a set of tableware and resell it after the wedding.

▶  Items like colored napkins and colored glassware will raise your rental costs. Stick to clear glassware and neutral linens and save.

## HEATERS

You may need to rent heaters if your ceremony or reception will be held outdoors and if the temperature could drop below 65 degrees.

**Options:** There are electric and gas heaters, both of which come in different sizes. Gas heaters are more popular since they do not have unsightly and unsafe electric cords.

**Price Range:** $25 - $75 each

► Consider setting up a firepit where guests can gather to keep warm, instead of renting heaters. For a rustic wedding, provide quilts and blankets.

## LANTERNS

Lanterns are often used at evening receptions to add soft lighting.

**Options:** Many choices are available, from fire lanterns to electric ones.

**Price Range:** $12 - $60

► For inexpensive paper lanterns that cost less than $1 each, shop OrientalTrading.com.

## MISCELLANEOUS RENTAL ITEMS

If your reception site or caterer doesn't provide them, you will need to purchase, rent, or borrow other miscellaneous items for your reception, such as trash cans, a gift table, trash bags, and so on.

**Rental Supplier:** _____ Contact: _____

Website: _____

E-mail: _____

Address: _____

City: _____ State: _____ Zip: _____

Phone: _____ Hours: _____

Payment Policy: _____

Cancellation Policy: _____

Delivery Time: _____ Tear-Down Time: _____

Setup Time: _____ Pickup Time: _____

| QTY. | ITEM | Description | Price | Total |
|------|------|-------------|-------|-------|
| | Arch/Altar | | $ | $ |
| | Canopy (Chuppah) | | $ | $ |
| | Backdrops | | $ | $ |
| | Floor Candelabra | | $ | $ |
| | Candles | | $ | $ |
| | Candle lighters | | $ | $ |
| | Kneeling Bench | | $ | $ |
| | Aisle Stanchions | | $ | $ |
| | Aisle Runners | | $ | $ |
| | Guest Book Stand | | $ | $ |
| | Gift Table | | $ | $ |
| | Chairs | | $ | $ |
| | Audio Equipment | | $ | $ |
| | Lighting | | $ | $ |
| | Heating/Cooling | | $ | $ |
| | Umbrellas/Tents | | $ | $ |
| | Bug Eliminator | | $ | $ |
| | Coat/Hat Rack | | $ | $ |
| | Garbage Cans | | $ | $ |

## RENTAL SUPPLIER COMPARISON CHART

| Questions | POSSIBILITY 1 |
|---|---|
| What is the name of the party rental supplier? | |
| What is the address of the party rental supplier? | |
| What is the web site and e-mail of the party rental supplier? | |
| What is the name and phone number of my contact person? | |
| How many years have you been in business? | |
| What are your hours of operation? | |
| Do you have liability insurance? | |
| What is the cost per item needed? | |
| What is the cost of pickup and delivery? | |
| What is the cost of setting up the items rented? | |
| When would the items be delivered? | |
| When would the items be picked up after the event? | |
| What is your payment policy? | |
| What is your cancellation policy? | |
| Other: | |
| Other: | |
| Other: | |

| POSSIBILITY 2 | POSSIBILITY 3 |
| --- | --- |
|  |  |
|  |  |
|  |  |
|  |  |
|  |  |
|  |  |
|  |  |
|  |  |
|  |  |
|  |  |
|  |  |
|  |  |
|  |  |
|  |  |
|  |  |
|  |  |
|  |  |

# RECEPTION EQUIPMENT CHECKLIST

**Rental Supplier:** _____ Contact: _____

Website: _____

E-mail: _____

Address: _____

City: _____ State: _____ Zip: _____

Phone: _____ Hours: _____

Payment Policy: _____

Cancellation Policy: _____

Delivery Time: _____ Tear-Down Time: _____

Setup Time: _____ Pickup Time: _____

| QTY. | ITEM | Description | Price | Total |
|------|------|-------------|-------|-------|
| | Audio Equipment | | $ | $ |
| | Cake Table | | $ | $ |
| | Candelabras/Candles | | $ | $ |
| | Canopies | | $ | $ |
| | Coat/Hat Rack | | $ | $ |
| | Dance Floor | | $ | $ |
| | Bug Eliminator | | $ | $ |
| | Garbage Cans | | $ | $ |
| | Gift Table | | $ | $ |
| | Guest Tables | | $ | $ |
| | Heating/Cooling | | $ | $ |
| | High/Booster Chairs | | $ | $ |
| | Lighting | | $ | $ |
| | Mirror Disco Ball | | $ | $ |
| | Place Card Table | | $ | $ |
| | Tents | | $ | $ |
| | Umbrellas | | $ | $ |
| | Visual Equipment | | $ | $ |
| | Wheelchair Ramp | | $ | $ |

# Catie & Ben

Total Spent: $7,140
March 20, 2010 • Gilbert, Arizona • 150 guests
Photography by Dana Grant, http://danagrantphotography.com

## Budget Breakdown

| | | | | |
|---|---|---|---|---|
| Attire | $388 | Bar | $250 |
| Stationery | $34 | Music | $21 |
| Ceremony & Reception Site | $0 | Bakery | $0 |
| | | Flowers | $800 |
| Photography | $2,800 | Décor & Rental Items | $1,100 |
| Videography | N/A | Miscellaneous | $490 |
| Food | $1,257 | Total | $7,140 |

Catie and Ben's 1940s-inspired backyard wedding was full of real vintage details — from an old photobooth the bride's brother converted to digital to the black-and-white Little Rascals and Shirley Temple movies playing on a screen throughout the evening. The couple was super-creative on a small budget, with thrift store and garage sale treasures making the bride's brother's backyard feel like a cozy living room full of their closest family and friends. "Every single person who came to our reception said it was exactly what they would have wanted, from my small-town cousins to big-city businessmen," said the bride. "Who would have thought my little thrift store wedding would have gotten so much attention!"

### FROM THE BRIDE

I wanted to spend as little money as possible and still have the wedding represent who we are. To get married in a big expensive venue that didn't have pieces of me everywhere wouldn't have had the same feeling.

When Ben proposed, I was actually saving for a big Europe trip, so it worked out that I had money to plan the wedding in only 3 months! I'm not a big spender anyway. I love thrift stores!

I wanted the wedding to have a backyard bed-and-breakfast feel. I started out with a 1940s theme, because I love that music and era, and then it sort of ended up being everything that I love shoved into one backyard.

## VENUE

We got married in my brother's backyard, so that was free! My brothers did all of the labor: putting up lights, building steps and arbors, painting the dance floor, and hanging chandeliers.

## STATIONERY

I printed my own wedding invitations. For $14, we bought 2 boxes of wedding invitations from the clearance rack at Target and used $20 in ink to print them.

## ATTIRE

Obviously, the biggest DIY project was my dress. I saw a picture of a dress that I loved and then was also inspired by the 1940s. I combined the two, and my mom was able to create it. She has been a professional seamstress for years. I bought the fabric at Mood on a trip to New York with my girlfriends. Ben wore a rented tux and the groomsmen wore $3 thrift store vests. Ben's mom made her own dress and the flower girl dress from leftover fabric from my dress.

## PHOTOGRAPHY

Our biggest splurge was on photography. This is where some might scrimp, but to me, a good photographer can make anything look good. And how sad to go through all the work to plan a wedding and not even have someone who can capture it all!

## CEREMONY

Ben's dad married us. When I came

around the corner down the aisle I could see Ben standing on his tippy toes peeking over heads trying to see me. When I got to the front, his eyes were all teary. So cute! He later whispered in my ear that he about lost it when he saw me come around the corner.

## DÉCOR

The backyard was made to look like we were inside a house — the chandeliers hanging from trees, the hinged doors, the couches, the dressers. We bought the window panes at a garage sale for $10. They came from a barn that had been torn down. The décor gave the reception such a warm feel.

My friend made most of the hat boxes that were used as centerpieces. We

used fabric and paper we already had and added some brooches. Some were my mother's brooches, some were my grandmother's, and others were from thrift stores. I also had a friend make a cute sign that had our names on it for when you walked into the reception.

Don't forget about lighting — it is so important! It sets the whole mood. I used large lightbulbs and covered them with paper lanterns. When the sun went down, it looked magical.

Probably the most fun detail of our wedding was the really old photobooth I found on Craigslist

for $300. My brother was able to convert it to digital by using my camera and his printer to make it just like a real photobooth. It was the biggest hit at the reception. Our guests still talk about it!

## FOOD & BAR

My sister and best friend made all the food. My sister made chicken and mashed potatoes the week before and froze them, then put them in big roasters on the wedding day. The chicken came out delicious and moist — who would have known? Friends and family made rolls, salad and green beans. They were served on mismatched plates from thrift stores, which were about $.50 each. Neighbors helped serve food all night. We didn't have a bar, just good old-fashioned soda.

## MUSIC

My brother is good with crowds so he acted as the DJ. It made it more personal, and he was free! I bought three 1940s albums on iTunes for $7 each and played them on an iPod and my brother's speakers. I love that style of music. It was so much fun and gave the reception a magical feel. My brother switched the music for different events.

We also had a huge screen playing 1940s black-and-white versions of Little Rascals and Shirley Temple movies all evening. Shirley Temple was my favorite growing up and Ben's was Little Rascals. The kids loved it!

## BAKERY

I love my friend's mom's cookies, so she made cookies. My sister makes fabulous crème brulee so she made that, as well as mini cupcakes. A friend of the family made tarts. My cousin had taken a cake-baking class; I showed her a picture and she created it! Nobody charged me. It was all their gifts to me.

## FLOWERS

I found a girl to do my flowers by word-of-mouth. She does flowers out of her house and charged a fraction of what a florist would have charged, and they looked every bit as good.

## ADVICE

Try to find used things or thrift store finds to put together. I was able to sell a lot of the cute stuff from my wedding afterward and recovered the money I spent on it. If you don't have an eye for making everything cute, find someone who does! There are so many talented people out there!

# Gifts

GIFTS ARE A WONDERFUL WAY TO SHOW your appreciation to family, friends, members of your wedding party, and to all those who have assisted you in your wedding planning process. Brides and grooms usually like to exchange something small yet meaningful. Keepsake items make wonderful gifts for members of the wedding party.

## BRIDE'S GIFT

The bride's gift is traditionally given by the groom to the bride. It is typically a personal gift, such as a piece of jewelry.

Options: A string of pearls, a watch, pearl earrings, jewelry box, perfume, or beautiful lingerie are nice gifts for the bride from her groom.

Price Range: $50 - $500

Ideas to Save Money: This gift is not necessary and should be given only if your budget allows. A letter with a personal note is a very special, yet inexpensive gift.

## GROOM'S GIFT

The groom's gift is traditionally given by the bride to the groom.

Options: A watch, cufflinks, a set of golf clubs, electronics, or a beautiful album of boudoir photos are nice gifts.

Price Range: $50 - $500

Ideas to Save Money: This gift is not necessary and should be given only if your budget allows. A letter from the bride proclaiming her love is a very special, yet inexpensive gift. Consider exchanging letters before the ceremony begins.

▶ "We decided to use Etsy.com for our gifts to each other and set a limit of $50. I got him typewriter-key cufflinks in his initials, and he had a custom drawing of the two of us made, which I framed and hung in our house."

~ Caitlin M., Roseville, MN

## BRIDESMAIDS' GIFTS

Bridesmaids' gifts are given by the bride to her bridesmaids and maid of honor as a permanent keepsake of the wedding.

**Options:** The perfect gift is jewelry or an accessory that can be worn both during and after the wedding. Choose earrings, a pashmina wrap, small clutch purse, or a hairpiece that complements your bridesmaids' dresses.

Other nice gift choices are a certificate for a spa treatment, personalized sweat suits or tank tops, favorite beauty products, a tote or cosmetic bag, and customized stationery.

**Things to Consider:** Bridesmaids' gifts are usually presented at the bridesmaids' luncheon, if there is one, or at the rehearsal dinner. The gift to the maid of honor may be similar to the bridesmaids' gifts, but should be a bit more expensive.

**Price Range:** $25 - $200 per gift

**Ideas to Save Money**

▶ Make bridesmaids a handmade gift, such as a hairpiece, earrings or other fun DIY project.

▶ Shop for deeply discounted gifts, such as pashminas and jewelry on sites like Overstock.com.

▶ Consider buying the bridesmaids' dresses as your gift to them. This will give you incentive to shop for an inexpensive dress or one on sale.

▶ "I have been in weddings where I felt like the bride picked fancy brides-maids' dresses with no regard for the people paying for them. For my wedding, I chose to gift my girls their dresses, which helped me keep some perspective on the cost. I ended up spending $300 for my 6 attendants, which was the same amount I would have spent on wedding party gifts anyway — plus I got brownie points with my girlfriends."
~ Kendall T., Phoenix, AZ

## USHERS' GIFTS

Ushers' gifts are given by the groom to his ushers as a permanent keepsake of the wedding.

**Options:** For ushers' gifts consider something they can wear during and after the wedding, such as a watch or cufflinks.

Other great gifts include a leather wallet, money clip, cigars, a personalized flask, luxury shaving kit, or a bottle of fine wine.

**Things to Consider:** The groom should deliver his gifts to the ushers at the rehearsal dinner or just before the wedding. The gift to the best man may be similar to the ushers' gifts, but should be a bit more expensive.

**Price Range:** $20 - $200 per gift

**Ideas to Save Money**

▶ Buy your ushers ties for the wedding. Nice ties can be inexpensive at stores like Marshall's and Nordstrom Rack, and ushers will wear them again.

▶ "My husband's friends are all outdoorsy types who like to go fishing, mountain biking, camping and rock climbing. For $20 each, he got his groomsmen lifetime memberships to REI, which gives them discounts, money back each year, and extras like free shipping. I thought it was a personal and unique gift they would use."

~ Abby J., Austin, TX

# Parties

WEDDINGS ARE OFTEN MUCH MORE THAN A day-long celebration. Some traditional events include the engagement party, bridal shower, bachelor and bachelorette parties, bridesmaids' luncheon, and rehearsal dinner. Some couples also like to have a brunch the day after the wedding to relax and relive the previous evening's celebration. You should include whatever celebrations fall within your budget.

## ENGAGEMENT PARTY

The engagement party is generally thrown by the bride's family to celebrate the big news. Gifts are not required at this party.

Options: An engagement party is typically held in your parents' home; however, renting a space or having dinner in a nice restaurant are also acceptable.

Things to Consider: If your schedule or budget won't allow for it, an engagement party is by no means a requirement.

## BRIDAL SHOWER

Traditionally, your wedding shower is thrown by your maid of honor and bridesmaids, unless they are a member of your immediate family. Because a shower is a gift-giving occasion, it is not considered socially acceptable for anyone in your immediate family to host this event. If your mother or sisters wish to be involved, have them offer to help with the cost of the event or offer their home for it. The agenda usually includes some games and gift-opening. Be sure to have someone keep track of which gift is from whom.

Options: Tea parties, spa days,

cocktail parties, and traditional at-home events are all options — these days even men are being invited as coed showers become more and more popular! Generally, an event is themed (lingerie, cooking, home décor), and the invitation should give guests an idea of what type of gift to bring.

**Things to Consider:** You may have several showers thrown for you. When creating your guest lists, be sure not to invite the same people to multiple showers (the exception being members of the wedding party, who may be invited to all showers without the obligation of bringing a gift.) Only include people who have been invited to the wedding — the only exception to this is a work shower, to which all coworkers may be invited, whether or not they are attending the wedding.

## BACHELOR PARTY

The bachelor party is a male-only affair typically organized by the best man. He is responsible for selecting the date and reserving the place and entertainment as well as inviting the groom's male friends and family. The ushers should also help with the organization of this party.

**Options:** A bachelor party can be as simple as a group of guys getting together for dinner and drinks, a day of golfing, a casino day trip, or a cruise. You might also attend a sporting event, brewery tour or tasting, or be adventurous and go skydiving or camping.

**Things to Consider:** You often hear wild stories about bachelor parties being nights full of women and alcohol, however, these types of events are actually quite rare. The bachelor party is simply a night for great friends and family to celebrate together.

Your best man should not plan the bachelor party for the night before the wedding, since you may consume a fair amount of alcohol and stay up late. You don't want to have a hangover or be exhausted during your wedding. Have the bachelor party two or three nights or even several months before the wedding.

Your best man should designate a driver for you and for those who will be drinking alcohol. Remember, you and your best man are responsible for the well-being of everybody invited to the party.

▶ Instead of spending a lot of money to fly and stay in another city, have the bachelor party in the same city as the wedding, in the days leading up to the event.

## BACHELORETTE PARTY

The bachelorette party is typically organized by the maid of honor for the females in the wedding party and any close family.

**Options:** Go out for dinner and drinks, have a spa day, go wine tasting, or on a day-cruise. Other fun options include a yoga or Pilates retreat, scavenger hunt, or a sporting event.

**Things to Consider:** The maid of honor should ask the bride what kind of party she wants — wild or mild. She should not plan the party for the night before the wedding, as you don't want to have a hangover or be exhausted during your wedding. A few weeks before or another date when the whole party can get together is more appropriate for the bachelorette party. You should also coordinate transportation for guests who are drinking.

The maid of honor should consider buying something funny or unique for the bride to wear to make her stand out, such as a feather boa, tiara, or beads.

▶ Consider having the bachelorette party in the same city as the wedding, in the days leading up to the wedding. Opt for something less expensive, such as a day at the nail salon or harbor tour.

**Real Couples' Weddings**

▶ "When I was the maid of honor in my friend's wedding, we were both on pretty tight budgets. Instead of a crazy bachelorette party, I took her to brunch, then booked four appointments for us and two other girls at a nice nail salon. They let me bring champagne and orange juice for mimosas, the hotel shuttle drove us to and from the salon, and it was good, inexpensive bonding time the day of the wedding."
~ Kathryn W., Knoxville, TN

## BRIDESMAIDS' LUNCHEON

The bridesmaids' luncheon is given by the bride for her bridesmaids. It is not a shower; rather, it is simply a time for good friends to get together formally before the bride changes her status from single to married.

Things to Consider: You can give your bridesmaids their gifts at this gathering. Otherwise, plan to give them their gifts at the rehearsal dinner.

Price Range: $12 - $60 per person

## REHEARSAL DINNER

It is customary that the groom's parents host a dinner party following the rehearsal, the evening before the wedding. The dinner usually includes the bridal party, their spouses or guests, both sets of parents, close family members, the officiant, and the wedding consultant and/or coordinator.

Options: The rehearsal dinner party can be held just about anywhere, from a restaurant, hotel, or private hall to the groom's parents' home.

Price Range: $10 - $100 per person

### Ideas to Save Money

▶ Restaurants specializing in Mexican, Japanese teppanyaki or gourmet pizza are fun yet inexpensive options.

### Real Couples' Weddings

▶ "A family friend offered her home for our rehearsal dinner, and we were happy not to have to rent a banquet room at a restaurant. We had about 25 people and did a wine dinner with cheese boards, fruit, cured meats, grilled bread and a selection of wines. It was informal but sophisticated, like our wedding, and allowed our guests and families to chat and get to know each other better."
~ Elizabeth M., Alexandria, VA

## DAY-AFTER WEDDING BRUNCH

Many times, the newlyweds will want to host a brunch the day after the wedding to spend one last bit of time with their guests and to thank them for coming to the wedding. Brunch can be much less formal than the rest of the wedding.

Options: You can have your caterer provide food for this event. If many guests are at one hotel, consider having the brunch there. If the hotel offers a continental breakfast, ask the hotel to reserve space in the breakfast room for your group.

Things to Consider: Choose a reasonable time for the brunch: Not too early, as many guests will be recovering from the festivities of the reception, but not too late, as out-of-town guests will have travel arrangements to attend to.

Price Range: $10 - $25 per person

### Ideas to Save Money

▶ Enlist family members to help cook or pick up brunch foods. A family member who still wants to contribute to your wedding is a perfect choice to host.

▶ Keep the menu simple and have bagels, muffins, croissants, jam, fruit, coffee, and juice.

### Real Couples' Weddings

▶ "A family friend kept asking how she could help, throughout our wedding planning. She used to work as a caterer and is a fabulous cook, so I asked her if she would be willing to make the food for a brunch the day after the wedding. Using the kitchen in the little house we rented, she whipped up a delicious meal. It was her gift to us for the wedding, and we couldn't have been happier. It was also really nice to spend some extra time with our guests who we don't see often."
~ Leslie P., Ithica, NY

# WEDDING PLANNING NOTES

# Julie & Guy

Total Spent: $4,775

**March 6, 2009 • Toronto, Canada • 52 guests**
**Photography by David Addington, http://davidaddington.ca**

## Budget Breakdown

| | | | |
|---|---|---|---|
| Attire | $600 | Bar | $550 |
| Stationery | $132 | Music | $42 |
| Ceremony & Reception Site | $580 | Bakery | $31 |
| | | Flowers | $190 |
| Photography | $0 | Décor & Rental Items | $0 |
| Videography | N/A | Miscellaneous | $450 |
| Food | $2,200 | Total | $4,775 |

Knitting lover Julie and her husband Guy were destined to have a wallet-friendly wedding from the start; after all, Guy proposed with a knitted engagement ring! Despite being told by many that an elegant $5,000 wedding was impossible, the couple celebrated in a beautiful historic venue with their nearest and dearest, dancing the night away until 1 a.m. An unfussy attitude and the help of friends and family meant that Julie and Guy were able to plan their perfect wedding-on-a-budget, in just 10 weeks! The bride even had time to knit her two maids of honor cashmere and mohair shawls. "Be flexible. Remind yourself that this is a party you are throwing to celebrate your marriage and your commitment to each other," Julie says. "Don't let the more upscale blogs and magazines make you wistful for a $100,000 budget. It doesn't cost much to have a super-fun wedding. Don't let anyone tell you differently."

## FROM THE BRIDE

Our dream was of a beautiful, traditional, intimate wedding on a small budget. We got engaged on Christmas Day and were married March 6. That's 2½ months! And honestly, I think it was the best choice. Having a shorter engagement meant that decisions had to be made quickly, and it helped keep things on-budget. I talked to some sites and caterers who said a $5,000 wedding couldn't be done. You can't see me right now, but I'm laughing out loud. We had an evening ceremony on a Friday night in downtown Toronto, with an open bar and hors d'oeuvres instead of a sit-down dinner. There were 54 people, including myself and my new husband.

## VENUE

I made a lot of inquiries into different venues and, in the end, we decided on a historical trust building that was so beautiful, it required very little decoration. I needed something that was attractive and large enough that it could comfortably contain 54 people, regardless of what the weather might be doing that day (March is always a little unpredictable). I added tea lights and flowers, and that's it! We also saved money because it was low season and a Friday. I was really up-front with the site manager about what my budget was, and what kind of bride I was (budget-conscious to the point of being Budgetzilla). And she was a dream — great to work with, accommodating when I made outrageous suggestions to cut costs, and really onboard with our vision.

## ATTIRE

Through the whole process, I told myself that the wedding gown was just a dress and focused mainly on the mermaid silhouette that I wanted. I searched OnceWed.com and PreownedWeddingDresses.com, which have hundreds of "once worn" wedding dresses for sale by their owners, and did searches based on my size. I got my dress from a really fantastic girl on Preowned-WeddingDresses.com. I got the dress, shipping, and customs duties all for $600. As for alterations, I did them myself, with the help of a friend.

I also made my own headband by sewing tiny pearl and crystal beads onto a plain white ribbon (75 cents), and attaching it to hair elastics. I'm really pleased with how it turned out. I bought silver shoes from Payless for $40. I'll definitely be wearing my fab silver shoes again!

## FOOD

Catering was where we spent the most time agonizing, and the most money. The biggest piece of advice I can offer on this subject is to check and see if your venue allows you to choose your own caterer, or if you have to choose from a tiny selection of ones that they work with. The site manager was up-front with me about having to use one of their caterers, but I had no idea

what that really meant. Catering can be so outrageously overpriced — and we were just having hors d'oeuvres! In the end, we got a great caterer that was not really on the list, (both the site and I did some compromising) and everything worked. People are still telling me that the food was fabulous, and I really love the fact that a restaurant, Bodega, did the catering. This means that any time we want, we can go there and eat the same or similar food, and remember our wedding night all over again. I know where I'm having dinner on my anniversary! If you are tight on funds, I really recommend the evening cocktail party approach.

## BAR

We had an open bar at the wedding, and decided to serve only wine and beer, but to have a selection. I bought 14 bottles of assorted red, 14 bottles of assorted white, and 5 cases of beer. The beer was in multipacks, which gave the guests options. We did run out of red wine; fortunately, we have great friends who keep bottles of wine in their trunk for emergencies, and one of our friends graciously brought in three more bottles of red.

## BAKERY

Let's face it — hardly any of your wedding cake gets eaten, no matter how delicious or terrible it is. I don't know why, but it's true. Thus, we were reluctant to spend $300 or more on a cake. My maids of honor and I chose to make cupcakes ourselves instead. We also built a great cupcake stand from cutout cardboard boxes that we covered in vinyl gift wrap, with white pots between the layers. The website AllThingsCupcake.com helped us figure out some of the details. Another friend revealed that her parents owned a bakery (start asking all your friends what their parents do for a living), and produced a perfect tiny wedding cake for our top tier, so that we had a cake to cut and something to put our bird cake topper on.

## RINGS

My ring cost $400 and was custom-made at a small independent jewelry store that also made my engagement ring (not my fabulous knitted one). I consider this to be another area where we really saved. If you go to a major jewelry chain, the markup is huge. They have a lot more overhead they need to pay for, and guess who's paying for that? You. The smaller store we visited was able to give us great service, handmade design, and really reasonable prices. Then we bought Guy's titanium ring off eBay.

## PHOTOGRAPHY

We skill-swapped with our photographer and saved there, as well. David was just starting out at the time and didn't have a website. Guy is a web designer who also does hosting, so our photographer got a website, and we got a photographer. Everybody wins.

## STATIONERY

Our dear friend Rebecca designed our gorgeous wedding invitations to represent our passions (mine: knitting; Guy's: rollerblading), and I loved the birds so much that they became the theme for the wedding. She also did the design for our programs and another friend printed them for us. I found that watercolor paper from an art supply store made for chic and cheap cardstock.

## FLOWERS

Think beyond flowers. Fresh flowers can be pretty expensive. The girl who owned my dress before me sent me a picture of her centerpieces, which were branches with paper blossoms and little lanterns on them. They were gorgeous. I thought that having some bare branches mixed in with the flowers would look very spring-y and fresh. I sent Guy out to trim the hedge in the yard and bring back branches. My maids of honor and I went to some local flower shops the morning of the wedding and bought what we needed. I deliberately didn't have a set flower in mind, so that I wouldn't end up making an emotional decision and get overpriced flowers. I opted for whatever looked good, fit the scheme, and was well-priced. We brought them to my kitchen and put together our bouquets and all the centerpieces.

I mixed in the branches Guy had cut with the floral arrangements, which filled them out beautifully. My maids of honor each carried a single stunning hydrangea bloom. It was perfect.

## MUSIC

Consider an iPod music list and get a friend to push the play button. We created three separate playlists — one for the wedding ceremony filler (classical music while guests were being seated), cocktail music (to play while the guests were drinking and socializing and we were getting photos done), and a dance playlist (for our First Dance and the subsequent shake-your-tailfeather party tunes that get the dance floor packed). We rented some speakers and a microphone for $42, and that was that.

## ADVICE

My bride-on-a-budget advice: First, DIY everything you can. We did our own flowers, our bouquets, the centerpieces, the cake stand, the cupcakes, the alterations, my headband, etc. People will say that you are adding to your stress. I say that starting out your life together deeply in debt from your wedding is far more stressful. Not to mention that a stress-free wedding is impossible, no matter how much money you spend!

Skill-swap as much as possible. Do you know a baker who would be willing to trade a handmade Norwegian fisherman's sweater for a wedding cake? Awesome. Get knitting.

Finally, it helps to remind yourselves that this day does not define who you are. Think about what kind of marriage you want and how you are going to achieve it, instead of obsessing over centerpieces, veils and napkin colors. In the end, I married the most wonderful man I have ever known. Guy is a fantastic husband, and I'm so ridiculously lucky.

# Legal Matters

WITH ALL THAT IS INVOLVED IN PLANNING a wedding, it is easy to forget some simple but necessary legal matters. Be sure that you don't forget to consider or complete some of the following items.

## MARRIAGE LICENSE

Marriage license requirements are state-regulated and may be obtained from the County Clerk in most county courthouses.

Options: Some states (California and Nevada, for example) offer two types of marriage licenses: a public license and a confidential one. The public license is the most common one and requires a health certificate and a blood test. It can only be obtained at the County Clerk's office.

The confidential license is usually less expensive and does not require a health certificate or blood test. If offered, it can usually be obtained from most Justices of the Peace. An oath must be taken in order to receive either license.

Things to Consider: Requirements vary from state to state, but generally include the following points:

1. Applying for and paying the fee for the marriage license. There is usually a waiting period before the license is valid and a limited time before it expires.

2. Meeting residency requirements for the state and/or county where the ceremony will take place.

3. Meeting the legal age requirements for both bride and groom or having parental consent.

4. Presenting any required identification, birth or baptismal certificates, marriage eligibility, or other documents.

5. Obtaining a medical examination and/or blood test for both the bride and groom to detect communicable diseases.

**Price Range:** $20 - $100

## PRENUPTIAL AGREEMENT

A prenuptial agreement is a legal contract between the bride and groom itemizing the property each brings into the marriage and explaining how those properties will be divided in case of divorce or death. Although you can write your own agreement, it is advisable to have an attorney draw up or review the document. The two of you should be represented by different attorneys.

**Things to Consider:** Consider a prenuptial agreement if one or both of you have a significant amount of capital or assets, or if there are children involved from a previous marriage. If you are going to live in a different state after the wedding, consider having an attorney from that state draw up or review your document.

Nobody likes to talk about divorce or death, but it is very important to give these issues your utmost consideration. By drawing a prenuptial agreement, you encourage open communication and get a better idea of each other's needs and expectations. You should also consider drawing up or reviewing your wills at this time.

**Price Range:** $500 - $3,000

**Ideas to Save Money**

▶ Some software packages allow you to write your own will and prenuptial agreement, which can save you substantial attorney's fees. However, if you decide to draw either agreement on your own, you should still have an attorney review it.

## TAXES

Don't forget to figure in the cost of taxes on all taxable items you purchase for your wedding. Many people make a big mistake by not figuring out the taxes they will have to pay for their wedding expenses.

For example, if you are planning a reception for 250 guests with an estimated cost of $60 per person for food and beverages, your pretax expenses would be $15,000. A sales tax of 7.5 percent would mean an additional expense of $1,125! Find out what the sales tax is in your area and which items are taxable and figure this expense into your overall budget.

# CHANGE OF ADDRESS WORKSHEET

| COMPANY | Account or Policy No. | Phone or Address | Done ✔ |
|---|---|---|---|
| Auto Insurance | | | |
| Auto Registration | | | |
| Bank Accounts | | | |
| 1) | | | |
| 2) | | | |
| Credit Cards | | | |
| 1) | | | |
| 2) | | | |
| 3) | | | |
| Dentist | | | |
| Doctors | | | |
| Driver's License | | | |
| Employee Records | | | |
| Insurance: Dental | | | |
| Insurance: Disability | | | |
| Insurance: Homeowner's | | | |
| Insurance: Life | | | |
| Insurance: Renter's | | | |
| Insurance: Other | | | |
| IRA Accounts | | | |
| 1) | | | |
| 2) | | | |
| 3) | | | |
| Leases | | | |
| 1) | | | |
| 2) | | | |
| Loan Companies | | | |
| 1) | | | |
| 2) | | | |
| 3) | | | |

| COMPANY | Account or Policy No. | Phone or Address | Done ✔ |
|---|---|---|---|
| Magazines | | | |
| Memberships | | | |
| 1) | | | |
| 2) | | | |
| 3) | | | |
| Mortgage | | | |
| Newspaper | | | |
| 1) | | | |
| 2) | | | |
| Passport | | | |
| Pensions | | | |
| Post Office | | | |
| Property Title | | | |
| Retirement Accounts | | | |
| 1) | | | |
| 2) | | | |
| Safe Deposit Box | | | |
| School Records | | | |
| 1) | | | |
| 2) | | | |
| 3) | | | |
| Social Security | | | |
| Stockbroker | | | |
| Taxes | | | |
| Telephone Company | | | |
| Utilities | | | |
| Voter Registration | | | |
| Will/Trust | | | |
| Other: | | | |
| Other: | | | |
| Other: | | | |
| Other: | | | |

## NAME AND ADDRESS CHANGE FORM

TO WHOM IT MAY CONCERN:

This is to inform you of my recent marriage and to request a change of name and/or address. This information will be effective as of:

My account/policy number is: _____

Under the name of: _____


**Previous Information:**

Husband's Name: _____ Phone: _____

Previous Address: _____

Wife's Maiden Name: _____ Phone: _____

Previous Address: _____


**New Information:**

Husband's Name: _____ Phone: _____

Wife's Name: _____ Phone: _____

New Address: _____


**Special Instructions:**
- ❑ Change name
- ❑ Change address/phone
- ❑ Add spouse's name
- ❑ Send necessary forms to include my spouse on my policy/account
- ❑ We plan to continue service
- ❑ We plan to discontinue service after: _____

If you have any questions, please feel free to contact us at: _____


Husband's Signature: _____

Wife's Signature: _____

# Wedding Party Responsibilities

EACH MEMBER OF YOUR WEDDING PARTY has his or her own individual duties and responsibilities. The following is a list of the most important duties for each member of your wedding party.

The most convenient method for conveying this information to members of your wedding party is by purchasing a set of the *Wedding Party Responsibility Cards*, published by WS Publishing Group.

These cards are attractive and contain all the information your wedding party needs to know to assure a smooth wedding: what to do, how to do it, when to do it, when to arrive, and much more. They also include financial responsibilities as well as the processional, recessional, and altar lineup.

This book is available at most major bookstores.

## MAID OF HONOR

- Helps bride select attire and address invitations.
- Plans bridal shower.
- Arrives at dressing site two hours before ceremony to assist bride in dressing.
- Arrives dressed at ceremony site one hour before the wedding for photographs.
- Arranges the bride's veil and train before the processional and recessional.
- Holds bride's bouquet and groom's ring, if no ring bearer, during the ceremony.
- Witnesses the signing of the marriage license.

- Keeps bride on schedule.
- Dances with best man during the bridal party dance.
- Helps bride change into her going away clothes.
- Mails wedding announcements after the wedding.
- Returns bridal slip, if rented.

## BEST MAN

- Responsible for organizing ushers' activities.
- Organizes bachelor party for groom.
- Drives groom to ceremony site and sees that he is properly dressed before the wedding.
- Arrives dressed at ceremony site one hour before the wedding for photographs.
- Brings marriage license to wedding.
- Pays the clergyman, musicians, photographer, and any other service providers the day of the wedding.
- Holds the bride's ring for the groom, if no ring bearer, until needed by officiant.
- Witnesses the signing of the marriage license.
- Drives newlyweds to reception, if no hired driver.
- Offers first toast at reception, usually before dinner.
- Keeps groom on schedule.
- Dances with maid of honor during the bridal party dance.
- May drive couple to airport or honeymoon suite.
- Oversees return of tuxedo rentals for groom and ushers, on time and in good condition.

## BRIDESMAIDS

- Assists maid of honor in planning bridal shower.
- Assists bride with errands and addressing invitations.
- Participates in all pre-wedding parties.
- Arrives at dressing site two hours before ceremony.
- Arrives dressed at ceremony site one hour before the wedding for photographs.
- Walks behind ushers in order of height during the processional, either in pairs or in single file.

- Sits next to ushers at the head table.
- Dances with ushers and other important guests.
- Encourages single women to participate in the bouquet toss.


## USHERS

- Helps best man with bachelor party.
- Arrives dressed at ceremony site one hour before the wedding for photographs.
- Distributes wedding programs and maps to the reception as guests arrive.
- Seats guests at the ceremony as follows:
    - If female, offer the right arm.
    - If male, walk along his left side.
    - If couple, offer right arm to female; male follows a step or two behind.
    - Seat bride's guests in left pews.
    - Seat groom's guests in right pews.
    - Maintain equal number of guests in left and right pews, if possible.
    - If a group of guests arrive at the same time, seat the eldest woman first.
    - Just prior to the processional, escort groom's mother to her seat; then escort bride's mother to her seat.
- Two ushers may roll carpet down the aisle after both mothers are seated.
- If pew ribbons are used, two ushers may loosen them one row at a time after the ceremony.
- Directs guests to the reception site.
- Dances with bridesmaids and other important guests.


## BRIDE'S MOTHER

- Helps prepare guest list for bride and her family.
- Helps plan the wedding ceremony and reception.
- Helps bride select her bridal gown.
- Helps bride keep track of gifts received.
- Selects her own attire according to the formality and color of thE wedding.

- Makes accommodations for bride's out-of-town guests.
- Arrives dressed at ceremony site one hour before the wedding for photographs.
- Is the last person to be seated right before the processional begins.
- Sits in the left front pew to the left of bride's father during the ceremony.
- May stand up to signal the start of the processional.
- Can witness the signing of the marriage license.
- Dances with the groom after the first dance.
- Acts as hostess at the reception.

## BRIDE'S FATHER

- Helps prepare guest list for bride and her family.
- Selects attire that complements groom's attire.
- Rides to the ceremony with bride in limousine.
- Arrives dressed at ceremony site one hour before the wedding for photographs.
- After giving bride away, sits in the left front pew to the right of bride's mother.
- If divorced, sits in second or third row unless financing the wedding.
- When officiant asks, "Who gives this bride away?" answers, "Her mother and I do," or something similar.
- Can witness the signing of the marriage license.
- Dances with bride after first dance.
- Acts as host at the reception.

## GROOM'S MOTHER

- Helps prepare guest list for groom and his family.
- Selects attire that complements mother of the bride's attire.
- Makes accommodations for groom's out-of-town guests.
- With groom's father, plans rehearsal dinner.
- Arrives dressed at ceremony site one hour before the wedding for photographs.
- May stand up to signal the start of the processional.
- Can witness the signing of the marriage license.

## GROOM'S FATHER

- Helps prepare guest list for groom and his family.
- Selects attire that complements groom's attire.
- With groom's mother, plans rehearsal dinner.
- Offers toast to bride at rehearsal dinner.
- Arrives dressed at ceremony site one hour before the wedding for photographs.
- Can witness the signing of the marriage license.


## FLOWER GIRL

- Usually between the ages of four and eight.
- Attends rehearsal to practice, but is not required to attend pre-wedding parties.
- Arrives dressed at ceremony site 45 minutes before the wedding for photos.
- Carries a basket filled with loose rose petals to strew along bride's path during processional, if allowed by ceremony site.
- If very young, may sit with her parents during ceremony.


## RING BEARER

- Usually between the ages of four and eight.
- Attends rehearsal to practice but is not required to attend pre-wedding parties.
- Arrives at ceremony site 45 minutes before the wedding for photographs.
- Carries a white pillow with rings attached.
- If younger than seven years, carries mock rings.
- If very young, may sit with his parents during ceremony.
- If mock rings are used, turns the ring pillow over at the end of the ceremony.

# WEDDING CONSULTANT'S INFORMATION FORM

*Make a copy of this form and give it to your wedding coordinator.*

| Parents | Name | Phone |
|---|---|---|
| Bride's Mother | | |
| Bride's Father | | |
| Groom's Mother | | |
| Groom's Father | | |
| Other: | | |
| Other: | | |

| Bride's Attendants | Name | Phone |
|---|---|---|
| Maid of Honor | | |
| Matron of Honor | | |
| Bridesmaid #1 | | |
| Bridesmaid #2 | | |
| Bridesmaid #3 | | |
| Bridesmaid #4 | | |
| Bridesmaid #5 | | |
| Bridesmaid #6 | | |
| Flower Girl | | |
| Other: | | |

| Groom's Attendants | Name | Phone |
|---|---|---|
| Best Man | | |
| Usher #1 | | |
| Usher #2 | | |
| Usher #3 | | |
| Usher #4 | | |
| Usher #5 | | |
| Usher #6 | | |
| Ring Bearer | | |
| Other: | | |

# Who Pays For What

CERTAIN PORTIONS OF THE WEDDING
are paid for by the bride and her family,
the groom and his family, the couple,
and the wedding party.

## BRIDE AND/OR BRIDE'S FAMILY

- Engagement party
- Wedding consultant's fee
- Bridal gown, veil, and accessories
- Wedding stationery, calligraphy, and postage
- Wedding gift for bridal couple
- Groom's wedding ring
- Gifts for bridesmaids
- Bridesmaids' bouquets
- Pre-wedding parties and bridesmaids' luncheon
- Photography and videography
- Bride's medical exam and blood test
- Wedding guest book and other accessories
- Total cost of the ceremony, including location, flowers, music, rental items, and accessories
- Total cost of the reception, including location, flowers, music, rental items, accessories, food, beverages, cake, decorations, favors, etc.
- Transportation for bridal party to ceremony and reception
- Own attire and travel expenses

## GROOM AND/OR GROOM'S FAMILY

- Own travel expenses and attire
- Rehearsal dinner
- Wedding gift for bridal couple

## BRIDE AND GROOM

- Bride's wedding ring
- Gifts for groom's attendants
- Medical exam for groom including blood test
- Bride's bouquet and going away corsage
- Mothers' and grandmothers' corsages
- All boutonnieres
- Officiant's fee
- Marriage license
- Honeymoon expenses

## ATTENDANTS

- Own attire except flowers
- Travel expenses
- Bridal shower paid for by maid of honor and bridesmaids
- Bachelor party paid for by best man and ushers
- Bachelorette party paid for by maid of honor and bridesmaids
- Wedding gift for bridal couple

# Jordyn & Bradley

Total Spent: $5,100
July 18, 2009 • Huntsville, Alabama • 200 guests
Photography by Tec Petaja, http://tecpetajaphoto.com

## Budget Breakdown

| | | | | |
|---|---|---|---|---|
| Attire | $1,000 | | Bar | $0 |
| Stationery | $200 | | Music | $0 |
| Ceremony & Reception Site | $1,000 | | Bakery | $0 |
| | | | Flowers | $400 |
| Photography | $0 | | Décor & Rental Items | $1,500 |
| Videography | $0 | | Miscellaneous | $0 |
| Food | $1,000 | | Total | $5,100 |

Who knew a simple jar of colorful buttons or a potted plant from Walmart could look so stunning, but Jordyn and Bradley's sweet Southern wedding proves that it's not what you spend but how you style it that makes a wedding beautiful and unique. To stick to a budget, they DIYed, borrowed, thrifted or used the help of friends for every element they could. Jordyn says, "Our style and taste is simple yet elegant, so it was easy to not get carried away with extravagant spending. Luckily, we live in a wonderful city with a low cost of living, too."

## FROM THE BRIDE

As soon as Bradley proposed, we began wedding dreaming and planning. While we didn't set out with a specific budget in mind, we did start to put back our pennies. We were married at Burritt on the Mountain in Huntsville, Alabama, where Bradley grew up. Since I'm the only girl in my

family, my parents and I were not very knowledgeable on wedding costs and how everything would really work out. Bradley and I both pitched in our separate incomes as well, so it was a group effort financially.

We wanted a wedding that was simple yet elegant without spending a fortune. I would say our biggest splurges were the location itself, Polaroid cameras and film for our guestbook, and the rentals, such as the tent, chairs, and tables. But the majority of our wedding was indeed DIY.

## PHOTOGRAPHY & VIDEOGRAPHY

Photography was one of the first things we thought of. Luckily, we ended up with Tec Petaja, who we had become close to. He is a dream photographer! We are so happy that he shot our wedding, and we adore the photos we'll have for a lifetime! A friend of ours also shot an 8mm film of the wedding as a gift.

## STATIONERY

We had our invitations screen-printed by friends of ours with a local business, and they gave us a great deal.

Simply Bloom Photography photographed our engagement session, and the photo on our fan programs is from their lovely shoot. Bradley's brother and sister-in-law printed our fan programs for us as a wedding gift from their promotional business, Bammer Jammer. We simply handwrote our family members and wedding party on the back of the fans.

## ATTIRE

My wedding dress is actually the first and only dress I ever tried on. I knew it was the perfect one, and I bought it right then and there because the boutique was running a killer sale that ended the next day. So my dress wasn't nearly as expensive as it could have been. My grandmother crocheted my headband by hand, and it is definitely one of my favorite and most sentimental details.

## FLOWERS

Our wedding was full of color and energy, mostly from the flowers. We purchased flowers from a local wholesale florist, and family and friends helped arrange all of the bouquets, corsages, table decorations, and so forth in the hours before the ceremony. We got potted plants from Walmart and put them in antique planters, vases, and glassware we had collected from thrift shops and borrowed from family members. We also collected vintage hankies and laundered them as favors, which was pretty inexpensive.

## MUSIC

A band or DJ was another big expense we were able to skip over. The cluster of vintage radios decorating our ceremony site was Bradley's wonderful idea, and we had classic wedding-themed music playing through them as guests entered the ceremony. We are great music lovers, and Bradley is a jamming DJ, if I do say so myself. We handpicked each and every song for the ceremony and reception and played them over Bradley's music equipment throughout the night.

## BAKERY & FOOD

Bradley's aunt made our cake as our wedding gift, and for dinner, we had chicken and dumplings, corn casserole, turnip greens, and cornbread

catered locally. To drink, we served tea, lemonade, and bottled orange cream sodas, root beer, and cokes. A good ol' Southern meal!

## ADVICE

Collect, borrow and thrift what you can. Look around you for ideas, help and support. I love living in the South surrounded by talented family, friends, and artists. We could not have had our perfect whimsical wedding day without them!

# Timelines

THE FOLLOWING SECTION INCLUDES two different timelines or schedule of events for your wedding day: one for members of your wedding party and one for the various service providers you have hired.

Use these timelines to help your wedding party and service providers understand their roles and where they need to be throughout your wedding day. This will also give you a much better idea of how your special day will unfold.

When preparing your timeline, first list the time that your wedding ceremony will begin. Then work forward or backwards, using the sample as your guide. The samples included give you an idea of how much time each event typically takes. But feel free to change the amount of time allotted for any event when customizing your own.

# SAMPLE WEDDING PARTY TIME

This is a sample wedding party timeline. To develop your own, use the blank form in this chapter. Once you have created your own timeline, make copies and give one to each member of your wedding party.

| TIME | DESCRIPTION | BRIDE | BRIDE'S MOTHER | BRIDE'S FATHER | MAID OF HONOR | BRIDESMAIDS | BRIDE'S FAMILY | GROOM | GROOM'S MOTHER | GROOM'S FATHER | BEST MAN | USHERS | GROOM'S FAMILY | FLOWER GIRL | RING BEARER |
|---|---|---|---|---|---|---|---|---|---|---|---|---|---|---|---|
| 2:00 PM | Manicurist appointment | ✓ | ✓ | | ✓ | ✓ | | | | | | | | | |
| 2:30 PM | Hair/makeup appointment | ✓ | ✓ | | ✓ | ✓ | | | | | | | | | |
| 4:15 PM | Arrive at dressing site | ✓ | ✓ | | ✓ | ✓ | | | | | | | | | |
| 4:30 PM | Arrive at dressing site | | | | | | | ✓ | | | ✓ | ✓ | | | |
| 4:45 PM | Pre-ceremony photos | | | | | | | ✓ | ✓ | ✓ | ✓ | ✓ | ✓ | | |
| 5:15 PM | Arrive at ceremony site | | | | | | | ✓ | ✓ | ✓ | ✓ | ✓ | ✓ | | |
| 5:15 PM | Pre-ceremony photos | ✓ | ✓ | ✓ | ✓ | ✓ | ✓ | | | | | | | | |
| 5:20 PM | Give officiant marriage license and fees | | | | | | | | | | ✓ | | | | |
| 5:20 PM | Ushers receive seating chart | | | | | | | | | | | ✓ | | | |
| 5:30 PM | Ushers distribute wedding programs | | | | | | | | | | | ✓ | | | |
| 5:30 PM | Arrive at ceremony site | | | | | | | | | | | | | ✓ | ✓ |
| 5:30 PM | Guest book attendant has guests sign book | | | | | | | | | | | | | | |
| 5:30 PM | Prelude music begins | | | | | | | | | | | | | | |
| 5:35 PM | Ushers begin seating guests | | | | | | | | | | | ✓ | | | |
| 5:45 PM | Arrive at ceremony site | ✓ | ✓ | ✓ | ✓ | ✓ | ✓ | | | | | | | | |
| 5:45 PM | Ushers seat honored guests | | | | | | | | | | | ✓ | | | |
| 5:50 PM | Ushers seat groom's parents | | | | | | | | ✓ | ✓ | | ✓ | | | |
| 5:55 PM | Ushers seat bride's mother | | ✓ | | | | | | | | | ✓ | | | |
| 5:55 PM | Attendants line up for procession | | | ✓ | ✓ | | | | | | | ✓ | | ✓ | ✓ |
| 5:56 PM | Bride's father takes his place next to bride | ✓ | | ✓ | | | | | | | | | | | |
| 5:57 PM | Ushers roll out aisle runner | | | | | | | | | | | ✓ | | | |
| 5:58 PM | Groom's party enters | | | | | | | ✓ | | | ✓ | | | | |
| 6:00 PM | Processional music begins | | | | | | | | | | | | | | |

| TIME | DESCRIPTION | BRIDE | BRIDE'S MOTHER | BRIDE'S FATHER | MAID OF HONOR | BRIDESMAIDS | BRIDE'S FAMILY | GROOM | GROOM'S MOTHER | GROOM'S FATHER | BEST MAN | USHERS | GROOM'S FAMILY | FLOWER GIRL | RING BEARER |
|---|---|---|---|---|---|---|---|---|---|---|---|---|---|---|---|
| 6:00 PM | Groom's mother rises | | | | | | | | ✓ | | | | | | |
| 6:01 PM | Ushers enter | | | | | | | | | | | ✓ | | | |
| 6:02 PM | Wedding party marches up aisle | ✓ | | ✓ | ✓ | ✓ | | | | | | | | ✓ | ✓ |
| 6:20 PM | Wedding party marches down aisle | ✓ | | | ✓ | | | ✓ | | | ✓ | | | ✓ | ✓ |
| 6:22 PM | Parents march down aisle | | ✓ | ✓ | | | | | ✓ | ✓ | | | | | |
| 6:25 PM | Sign marriage certificate | ✓ | | | ✓ | | | ✓ | | | ✓ | | | | |
| 6:30 PM | Post-ceremony photos taken | ✓ | ✓ | ✓ | ✓ | ✓ | ✓ | ✓ | ✓ | ✓ | ✓ | ✓ | ✓ | ✓ | ✓ |
| 6:30 PM | Cocktails and hors d'oeuvres served | | | | | | | | | | | | | | |
| 6:30 PM | Gift attendant watches gifts as guests arrive | | | | | | | | | | | | | | |
| 7:15 PM | DJ announces entrance/receiving line forms | ✓ | | | | | | ✓ | | | | | | | |
| 7:45 PM | Guests are seated and dinner is served | | | | | | | | | | | | | | |
| 8:30 PM | Toasts are given | | | | | | | | | | ✓ | | | | |
| 8:40 PM | First dance | ✓ | | | | | | ✓ | | | | | | | |
| 8:45 PM | Traditional dances | ✓ | ✓ | ✓ | | | | ✓ | ✓ | ✓ | | | | | |
| 9:00 PM | Open dance floor for all guests | | | | | | | | | | | | | | |
| 9:30 PM | Bride and groom toast before cutting cake | ✓ | | | | | | ✓ | | | | | | | |
| 9:40 PM | Cake-cutting ceremony | ✓ | | | | | | ✓ | | | | | | | |
| 10:00 PM | Bride tosses bouquet to single women | ✓ | | | ✓ | ✓ | | | | | | | | ✓ | |
| 10:10 PM | Groom removes garter from bride's leg | ✓ | | | | | | ✓ | | | | | | | |
| 10:15 PM | Groom tosses garter to single men | | | | | | | ✓ | | | ✓ | ✓ | | | ✓ |
| 10:20 PM | Place garter on woman's leg | | | | | | | | | | | | | | |
| 10:30 PM | Distribute flower petals to toss over couple | | | | | | | | | | | | | | |
| 10:45 PM | Bride and groom make grand exit | ✓ | | | | | | ✓ | | | | | | | |

# WEDDING PARTY TIMELINE

Create your own timeline using this form. Make copies and give one to each member of your wedding party.

| TIME | DESCRIPTION | BRIDE | BRIDE'S MOTHER | BRIDE'S FATHER | MAID OF HONOR | BRIDESMAIDS | BRIDE'S FAMILY | GROOM | GROOM'S MOTHER | GROOM'S FATHER | BEST MAN | USHERS | GROOM'S FAMILY | FLOWER GIRL | RING BEARER |
|---|---|---|---|---|---|---|---|---|---|---|---|---|---|---|---|
| | | | | | | | | | | | | | | | |
| | | | | | | | | | | | | | | | |
| | | | | | | | | | | | | | | | |
| | | | | | | | | | | | | | | | |
| | | | | | | | | | | | | | | | |
| | | | | | | | | | | | | | | | |
| | | | | | | | | | | | | | | | |
| | | | | | | | | | | | | | | | |
| | | | | | | | | | | | | | | | |
| | | | | | | | | | | | | | | | |
| | | | | | | | | | | | | | | | |
| | | | | | | | | | | | | | | | |
| | | | | | | | | | | | | | | | |
| | | | | | | | | | | | | | | | |
| | | | | | | | | | | | | | | | |
| | | | | | | | | | | | | | | | |
| | | | | | | | | | | | | | | | |
| | | | | | | | | | | | | | | | |
| | | | | | | | | | | | | | | | |
| | | | | | | | | | | | | | | | |
| | | | | | | | | | | | | | | | |
| | | | | | | | | | | | | | | | |
| | | | | | | | | | | | | | | | |

| TIME | DESCRIPTION | BRIDE | BRIDE'S MOTHER | BRIDE'S FATHER | MAID OF HONOR | BRIDESMAIDS | BRIDE'S FAMILY | GROOM | GROOM'S MOTHER | GROOM'S FATHER | BEST MAN | USHERS | GROOM'S FAMILY | FLOWER GIRL | RING BEARER |
|------|-------------|-------|----------------|----------------|---------------|-------------|----------------|-------|----------------|----------------|----------|--------|----------------|-------------|-------------|
| | | | | | | | | | | | | | | | |
| | | | | | | | | | | | | | | | |
| | | | | | | | | | | | | | | | |
| | | | | | | | | | | | | | | | |
| | | | | | | | | | | | | | | | |
| | | | | | | | | | | | | | | | |
| | | | | | | | | | | | | | | | |
| | | | | | | | | | | | | | | | |
| | | | | | | | | | | | | | | | |
| | | | | | | | | | | | | | | | |
| | | | | | | | | | | | | | | | |
| | | | | | | | | | | | | | | | |
| | | | | | | | | | | | | | | | |
| | | | | | | | | | | | | | | | |
| | | | | | | | | | | | | | | | |
| | | | | | | | | | | | | | | | |
| | | | | | | | | | | | | | | | |
| | | | | | | | | | | | | | | | |
| | | | | | | | | | | | | | | | |
| | | | | | | | | | | | | | | | |
| | | | | | | | | | | | | | | | |
| | | | | | | | | | | | | | | | |
| | | | | | | | | | | | | | | | |

# SAMPLE SERVICE PROVIDER TIMELINE

This is a sample of a service provider timeline. To develop your own, use the blank form in this chapter; then make copies and give one to each one of your service providers.

| TIME | DESCRIPTION | BAKER | CATERER | CEREMONY MUSICIANS | OFFICIANT | OTHER | FLORIST | HAIRSTYLIST | LIMOUSINE | MAKEUP ARTIST | MANICURIST | PARTY RENTALS | PHOTOGRAPHER | RECEPTION MUSICIANS | VIDEOGRAPHER |
|---|---|---|---|---|---|---|---|---|---|---|---|---|---|---|---|
| 1:00 PM | Supplies delivered to ceremony site | | | | | | | | | | | ✓ | | | |
| 1:30 PM | Supplies delivered to reception site | | | | | | | | | | | ✓ | | | |
| 2:00 PM | Manicurist meets bride at: | | | | | | | | | | ✓ | | | | |
| 2:30 PM | Makeup artist meets bride at: | | | | | | | | | ✓ | | | | | |
| 3:00 PM | Hairstylist meets bride at: | | | | | | | ✓ | | | | | | | |
| 4:00 PM | Limousine picks up bridal party at: | | | | | | | | ✓ | | | | | | |
| 4:15 PM | Caterer begins setting up | | ✓ | | | | | | | | | | | | |
| 4:30 PM | Florist arrives at ceremony site | | | | | | ✓ | | | | | | | | |
| 4:40 PM | Baker delivers cake to reception site | ✓ | | | | | | | | | | | | | |
| 4:45 PM | Florist arrives at reception site | | | | | | ✓ | | | | | | | | |
| 4:45 PM | Pre-ceremony photos of groom's family at: | | | | | | | | | | | | ✓ | | |
| 5:00 PM | Videographer arrives at ceremony site | | | | | | | | | | | | | | ✓ |
| 5:15 PM | Pre-ceremony photos of bride's family at: | | | | | | | | | | | | ✓ | | |
| 5:20 PM | Ceremony site decorations finalized | | | | ✓ | ✓ | | | | | | | | | |
| 5:30 PM | Prelude music begins | | | ✓ | | | | | | | | | | | |
| 5:45 PM | Reception site decorations finalized | | ✓ | | ✓ | ✓ | | | | | | | | | |
| 5:58 PM | Officiant enters | | | | ✓ | | | | | | | | | | |
| 6:00 PM | Processional music begins | | | ✓ | | | | | | | | | | | |
| 6:15 PM | Caterer finishes setting up | | ✓ | | | | | | | | | | | | |
| 6:25 PM | Sign marriage certificate | | | | ✓ | | | | | | | | ✓ | | ✓ |
| 6:30 PM | Post-ceremony photos at: | | | | | | | | | | | | ✓ | | |
| 6:30 PM | Cocktails and hors d'oeuvres served | | ✓ | | | | | | | | | | | | |
| 6:30 PM | Band or DJ begins playing | | | | | | | | | | | | | ✓ | |

| TIME | DESCRIPTION | BAKER | CATERER | CEREMONY MUSICIANS | OFFICIANT | OTHER | FLORIST | HAIRSTYLIST | LIMOUSINE | MAKEUP ARTIST | MANICURIST | PARTY RENTALS | PHOTOGRAPHER | RECEPTION MUSICIANS | VIDEOGRAPHER |
|---|---|---|---|---|---|---|---|---|---|---|---|---|---|---|---|
| 6:30 PM | Transport guest book/gifts to reception site | | | | | ✓ | | | | | | | | | |
| 6:45 PM | Move arch/urns/flowers to reception site | | | | | ✓ | | | | | | | | | |
| 7:00 PM | Limo picks up bride/groom at ceremony site | | | | | | | | ✓ | | | | | | |
| 7:15 PM | DJ announces entrance of bride and groom | | | | | | | | | | | | | ✓ | |
| 7:45 PM | Dinner is served | | ✓ | | | | | | | | | | | | |
| 8:15 PM | Champagne served for toasts | | ✓ | | | | | | | | | | | | |
| 8:30 PM | Band/DJ announces toast by best man | | | | | | | | | | | | | ✓ | |
| 8:40 PM | Band/DJ announces first dance | | | | | | | | | | | | | ✓ | |
| 9:00 PM | Transport gifts to: | | | | | ✓ | | | | | | | | | |
| 9:30 PM | Band/DJ announces cake-cutting ceremony | | | | | | | | | | | | | ✓ | |
| 10:30 PM | Transport top tier of cake, cake-top, etc. to: | | | | | ✓ | | | | | | | | | |
| 10:40 PM | Transport rental items to: | | | | | ✓ | | | | | | | | | |
| 10:45 PM | Limo picks up bride/groom at reception site | | | | | | | | ✓ | | | | | | |
| 11:00 PM | Videographer departs | | | | | | | | | | | | | | ✓ |
| 11:00 PM | Photographer departs | | | | | | | | | | | | ✓ | | |
| 11:00 PM | Wedding consultant departs | | | | | ✓ | | | | | | | | | |
| 11:30 PM | Band/DJ stops playing | | | | | | | | | | | | | ✓ | |
| 11:45 PM | Picks up supplies at ceremony/reception sites | | | | | | | | | | | ✓ | | | |

## SERVICE PROVIDER TIMELINE

Create your own timeline using this form. Make copies and give one to each of your service providers.

| TIME | DESCRIPTION | BAKERY | CATERER | CEREMONY MUSICIANS | OFFICIANT | OTHER | FLORIST | HAIRSTYLIST | LIMOUSINE | MAKEUP ARTIST | MANICURIST | PARTY RENTALS | PHOTOGRAPHER | RECEPTION MUSICIANS | VIDEOGRAPHER |
|---|---|---|---|---|---|---|---|---|---|---|---|---|---|---|---|
| | | | | | | | | | | | | | | | |
| | | | | | | | | | | | | | | | |
| | | | | | | | | | | | | | | | |
| | | | | | | | | | | | | | | | |
| | | | | | | | | | | | | | | | |
| | | | | | | | | | | | | | | | |
| | | | | | | | | | | | | | | | |
| | | | | | | | | | | | | | | | |
| | | | | | | | | | | | | | | | |
| | | | | | | | | | | | | | | | |
| | | | | | | | | | | | | | | | |
| | | | | | | | | | | | | | | | |
| | | | | | | | | | | | | | | | |
| | | | | | | | | | | | | | | | |
| | | | | | | | | | | | | | | | |
| | | | | | | | | | | | | | | | |
| | | | | | | | | | | | | | | | |
| | | | | | | | | | | | | | | | |
| | | | | | | | | | | | | | | | |
| | | | | | | | | | | | | | | | |
| | | | | | | | | | | | | | | | |

# SERVICE PROVIDER TIMELINE

| TIME | DESCRIPTION | BAKERY | CATERER | CEREMONY MUSICIANS | OFFICIANT | OTHER | FLORIST | HAIRSTYLIST | LIMOUSINE | MAKEUP ARTIST | MANICURIST | PARTY RENTALS | PHOTOGRAPHER | RECEPTION MUSICIANS | VIDEOGRAPHER |
|------|-------------|--------|---------|--------------------|-----------|-------|---------|-------------|-----------|---------------|------------|---------------|--------------|---------------------|--------------|
| | | | | | | | | | | | | | | | |
| | | | | | | | | | | | | | | | |
| | | | | | | | | | | | | | | | |
| | | | | | | | | | | | | | | | |
| | | | | | | | | | | | | | | | |
| | | | | | | | | | | | | | | | |
| | | | | | | | | | | | | | | | |
| | | | | | | | | | | | | | | | |
| | | | | | | | | | | | | | | | |
| | | | | | | | | | | | | | | | |
| | | | | | | | | | | | | | | | |
| | | | | | | | | | | | | | | | |
| | | | | | | | | | | | | | | | |
| | | | | | | | | | | | | | | | |
| | | | | | | | | | | | | | | | |
| | | | | | | | | | | | | | | | |
| | | | | | | | | | | | | | | | |
| | | | | | | | | | | | | | | | |
| | | | | | | | | | | | | | | | |
| | | | | | | | | | | | | | | | |
| | | | | | | | | | | | | | | | |
| | | | | | | | | | | | | | | | |
| | | | | | | | | | | | | | | | |
| | | | | | | | | | | | | | | | |
| | | | | | | | | | | | | | | | |

# WEDDING PLANNING NOTES

..................................................................................................

..................................................................................................

..................................................................................................

..................................................................................................

..................................................................................................

..................................................................................................

..................................................................................................

..................................................................................................

..................................................................................................

..................................................................................................

..................................................................................................

..................................................................................................

..................................................................................................

..................................................................................................

..................................................................................................

..................................................................................................

..................................................................................................

..................................................................................................

..................................................................................................

..................................................................................................

# Adrienne & Michael

Total Spent: $10,000
October 4, 2008 • Philadelphia, Pennsylvania • 130 guests
Photography by Kelli Cohee, www.kellicohee.com

## Budget Breakdown

| | | | | |
|---|---|---|---|---|
| Attire | $1,520 | Bar | $400 |
| Stationery | $70 | Music | $1,350 |
| Ceremony & Reception Site | $0 | Bakery | N/A |
| | | Flowers | $269 |
| Photography | $700 | Décor & Rental Items | $500 |
| Videography | N/A | Miscellaneous | $548 |
| Food | $4,643 | Total | $10,000 |

Although Adrienne claims to be the girl who never imagined her wedding day, she and Michael succeeded in planning a backyard barbecue full of the elements most important to them: "Music, drink, friends, and family ... the key ingredients to a good party!" "That's really what we wanted — a good ol' party," explains the bride, "One at which two people happen to be joining together in holy matrimony." By prioritizing and tackling a few DIY projects, this creative couple — who met when Michael sang a song Adrienne wrote as a duet — stuck right to their $10,000 budget ... without missing a beat.

## FROM THE BRIDE

Our budget for the wedding was $10,000 and while it was challenging to keep it under that amount, it *is* doable. We had no elaborate plans or ideas for the wedding. The only thing I ever wanted was a barbecue in someone's backyard, and we were fortunate enough to have dear friends donate the beauty of their backyard for our day. The home sits on an old Philadelphia suburb estate, which has its own sad love story of a wealthy heiress falling in love with one of the estate's workers. The love was forbidden and the lovesick heiress threw herself to her death from the family's second story home. The story goes that occasionally one can view the ghost of a mourning grandmother rocking in her chair in front of the second story window. I'd like to think she was smiling down on us as we married under the old oak tree in her front yard.

## ATTIRE

My dress was Priscilla of Boston. It was the splurge that initially sent us over our budget, but I was able to sell my dress after the wedding, which kept us at $10,000 once again. I bought my jewelry from Etsy and adorned my shoes with vintage rhinestone clip-on earrings from eBay. Michael wore a suit from Express and shoes by Steve Madden.

## CEREMONY

Our wedding day was beautiful — and a good thing, because we had *no* weather contingency plan. We strung 20 yards of white fabric (only about $1 per yard!) from branch to branch of the ceremonial oak tree to create an organic, angelic feeling. For the ceremony, guests spread themselves out on the front yard, sitting in chairs, the grass, and some even sat atop a wooden fence that had been decorated by a garland of greenery that my mom created by salvaging ivy that a neighbor was throwing away.

## FLOWERS

Flowers were purchased by a wholesaler and my sister designed the bouquets, which doubled as table centerpieces (I mean, really, does any bridesmaid know what happens to her bouquet after a couple drinks? Why not have it serve two purposes?). My mom created the boutonnieres and corsages.

## DÉCOR

Tables were covered in white table cloths and topped with black and white polkadot squares. White daisies, mums, and sunflowers filled antique mason jars, and votives borrowed from my sister's wedding provided candlelight as the sun went down. We

strung thousands of twinkling white lights around the pool to establish a dance floor on the courtyard for our guests to get their groove on.

I come from a long line of DIYers, before there was even an acronym for it. Sure, most do-it-yourselfing is necessary from a financial perspective, but there's also the desire to have a certain level of quality control that you can't always get unless you do it yourself. Remember the old saying: "If you want something done right, you gotta do it yourself"? For instance, the trees surrounding our reception were adorned with mason jar lanterns hanging from twine in the branches. Buy mason jars from a crafts store and, using high-gauge wire, cut a piece about 14 inches long. Connect the ends by twisting them together. Place the jar in the middle of the wire circle. Form the wire loop around the mouth of the jar to create handles on the sides. Pull handles upward and loop another wire piece through the handles, so you can attach twine far enough away from the flame that you don't have to worry about fire.

## FOOD

We opted not to have a formal sit-down dinner, because no one ever really

wants cocktail hour to end! We hired a local caterer to serve up barbecue and rented a tent for folks to sit down and eat. Our tent was decorated with about 40 tissue paper flowers, like the kind I remember making in Girl Scouts (or Martha Stewart can show you how).

## BAKERY

We had our caterer make pies instead of a wedding cake and set up a candy bar, which the children raided before

I even made it down the aisle! We bought a variety of jars from IKEA, then we filled them with all kinds of fun candy — wax lips, Mary Janes, Red Vines, Necco wafers, and Lemonheads. I purchased a bunch of white sandwich bags and stamped them with our name and wedding date. The candy was a hit!

## MUSIC

Michael and I met through music. We sung a duet together (very love story). It was a song I wrote that was yearning for another voice. So, it was important to me that not only would good music be a part of our wedding day, but that our musically gifted friends were a part of the day as well. Our First Dance song was performed and written by a local Philadelphia area musician, John Conahan. The Hoppin John Orchestra also served as musical entertainment.

## FAVORS

My mom makes fantastic granola; I have never had better. For the wedding, she cooked 15 pounds of granola, and we filled 100 red Chinese take-out containers (bought from eBay), then tagged them with our names, wedding date, and "Mimi's Homemade Granola." Guests loved the little snack on the way home.

## ADVICE

I had quite a few caterers laugh at me when I told them my budget. I found that as soon as you say "wedding," it costs another $50 per person, so I stopped calling it a wedding and began referring to it as a party with 130 guests. I think I finally told my caterer that it was a wedding a week before the date!

There is no doubt that planning, preparing, and running a wedding yourself is a labor of love, but our wedding had the signature of all our loved ones, and that is priceless.

# WEDDING PLANNING NOTES

# WEDDING PLANNING NOTES

.............................................................................................................................

.............................................................................................................................

.............................................................................................................................

.............................................................................................................................

.............................................................................................................................

.............................................................................................................................

.............................................................................................................................

.............................................................................................................................

.............................................................................................................................

.............................................................................................................................

.............................................................................................................................

.............................................................................................................................

.............................................................................................................................

.............................................................................................................................

.............................................................................................................................

.............................................................................................................................

.............................................................................................................................

.............................................................................................................................

.............................................................................................................................

.............................................................................................................................

.............................................................................................................................

## WEDDING PLANNING NOTES

# WeddingSolutions.com

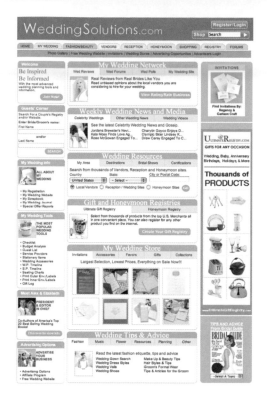

## Everything You Need to Plan Your Dream Wedding

- The Latest Wedding Gowns
- Comprehensive Wedding Planning Tools
- Articles, Tips & Advice
- Thousands of Local Vendors
- Beautiful Reception Sites
- Honeymoon Destinations
- Largest Online Wedding Store
- Wedding Forums
- Personal Wedding Website
- Honeymoon & Gift Registry
- Polls, News, Videos, Media
- Wedding Planning Certification Programs

## SEARCH FOR WEDDING GOWNS

### View the Latest Designs

Search for your perfect wedding gown by designer, style and price.

## SEARCH FOR WEDDING GOWNS

### Reputable & Reliable

Find local vendors, reception, honeymoon & destination wedding sites.

Log on to www.WeddingSolutions.com for more information

# WedSpace.com

## THE BEST WAY TO PLAN YOUR ENTIRE WEDDING!

# WedSpace.com

# FREE Online Wedding Journal!
# $29.95 Value

A fun and exciting way to share your Love Story
and Wedding Details with friends and family.

### *Celebrating the Wedding of*

## Chelsea & Trever

### June 10th, 2011 • 348 days to go!

Friend Request   Send to Friend   Send Message   Send E-Card   Invite to Group   Add to Favorites

HOME     OUR STORY     WEDDING DETAILS     REGISTRY     RSVP     MEDIA     VIEW OUR

**Welcome to our Wedding Journal!**

To read our love story, view our wedding details, see where we have registered, RSVP and so much more,
simply log in or register and click on "Friend Request." You will be able to read our Wedding Wall/blog, meet
our wedding vendors and other guests who are coming to the wedding, and so much more.

Answer quick questions and upload photos and videos
to customize pages including:

- All About Him
- All About Her
- How We Met
- Our Engagement

- Ceremony Details
- Reception Details
- Where to Stay
- And much more

## The perfect tool for your guests to RSVP for your wedding and find out where you have registered!

## Create Your FREE Online Wedding Journal Today!
### (Use discount code "FREE3369" during registration)